*Reel Deep in Montana's Rivers*

# REEL DEEP

## in Montana's Rivers

## JOHN HOLT

PRUETT PUBLISHING COMPANY
BOULDER, COLORADO

Printed in the United States
10 9 8 7 6 5 4 3 2 1

Library of Congress Cataloging-in-Publication Data

Holt, John, 1951–
    Reel deep in Montana's rivers / John Holt.
        p.    cm.
    Includes bibliographical references (p.   ) and index.
    ISBN 0-87108-832-0 (HC : acid-free paper)
    1. Fly fishing—Montana. 2. Rivers—Montana—Guidebooks.
I. Title.
SH456.H615      1993
799.1′755—dc20                                              93-8660
                                                               CIP


Cover and book design by Jody Chapel, Cover to Cover Design,
Denver, Colorado

Some of the information contained in this book was obtained while the
author researched articles for *American Angler, Fly Fisherman,* and *Fly
Rod & Reel* magazine.

Permission to reprint a portion of "Seasonable Angler," from the December
1992 issue of *Fly Fisherman* magazine, generously granted by Nick Lyons.
Copyright © 1992 by Nick Lyons.

*For Bob Jones*

there is a familiar stream

that struts its flow with style

and in the case of a long time fool

it is that old trout madness

that creates pleasure in a freak

who jumps to the mayfly rag

# Contents

# Acknowledgments

A fine aspect of fly fishing is the quality people one has the chance to come in contact with during the course of a year. Some of the finest include Wayne Hadley, Tom Weaver, Scott Rumsey, Bill Gardner, Bruce Rehwinkel, Ron Spoon, Don Peters, Liter Spence, Chris Clancy, and Phil Stewart, all of the Montana Department of Fish, Wildlife and Parks. Others who helped with the project directly or indirectly are Tom Rosenbauer of Orvis, Jim Pruett and Dianne Russell of Pruett Publishing Company, John Randolph, Marshall Bloom, Bob Buzzas, Dianne McDermand, Powell and Tazun, Ruth Welling, and Tony Acerrano. The following is a rogue's gallery of the friends and family I was able to spend some time fishing (or at least talking fishing) with this past season: John Talia, Mike Brennan, Tim Joern, Blanche and Chuck Johnson, Herb Rosene and Anne Wells, Ken Welles, Barry Serviente, aero commander Steve Welles, Stan Bradshaw, and Gary LaFontaine. Lastly, I would like to recognize the understanding exhibited by the individuals who make my life worth living— Jack, Elizabeth, Rachel, and Lynda, of course.

# Introduction: *Somewhere Down the Crazy River*

$S$tand anywhere long enough and you begin to start moving, slowly at first, but the pace accelerates to a speed well beyond control.

Winter in northwest Montana is like this. By mid-January the lack of fly fishing has reached terminal velocity, not just for me but for my friends too. Fly rods, reels, boxes of small Olives and Woolly Buggers are strewn all over the place from the rooms of my home to the rooms of my buddies' homes. This is a sad mess but one we all try and cope with each cold, mean season.

I call people I know scattered around the country and they call me, the frequency increasing in a nice synchronous rhythm with the accumulating snow outside my frosty windows. The days are short and mostly dark. A fire burns in the stove. I read a lot and daydream and write less and less. Next year's fishing is not really any closer, but sharing the frustration that comes with inaction and the winter dead-time-blues helps a bit.

One morning and many dollars in phone toll charges later, I learn that it's still cold in Vermont, the snow is flying down in Missoula, there's fog in San Mateo, no one is going outside in Minneapolis, the wind is howling in Deer Lodge, and the redfish are near shore down in Boca Grande. This sort of silliness appears to have the durability associated with infinity.

God! Where's March?

Then, for some reason, someone takes pity on us up here in the mountains and winter dies a sudden death in late January.

The days are sunny and in the forties. Nights rarely dip below twenty. Balmy weather for this time of the year, and I'm out casting a new 3-weight in the compacting snow. Browns are rising steadily along the bank piled up by the plow after last week's breezy white-out. A nice cutthroat just bulged over by the buried greenhouse. And some good rainbows are stacked up along the drift across the road by the mailbox. Damn good fishing in this state wherever you look.

February is springlike with a couple of days crowding the sixties, lots of sun, and the hint of spring's first warm zephyrs. Keep on hoping. Always hoping. Things will improve soon. I go fishing on the Flathead River a few times, taking lots of mountain whitefish and a few sluggish rainbows on Gold-Ribbed Hare's Ears connected to the end of a ratty leader left from last November. The bug drifts slowly through rocky runs down into dark pools. The whitefish are eager but the trout act like passed-out drunks rousted from an alley before daybreak by a sadistic Chicago cop.

And then it's March and the Skwala hatch on the Bitterroot with its good, colorful fish and the tantalizing promise of another year spent chasing trout all over the place. And that is what this book is all about: fishing some rivers I know very well, some I know a little bit, and some I know only slightly but that seem like recognizable strangers—an "I can't remember your name, but the face sure looks familiar; let's shoot the breeze for a while" type of situation.

Since the release of the first two books in this peripatetic three-book sequence (*Knee Deep in Montana's Trout Streams* and *Waist Deep in Montana's Lakes*), many people have offered opinions on my selections of rivers and lakes discussed in the books. Some say things to the effect that they have enjoyed the writing, others say I've been too easy on those who are raping Montana for a quick buck, and, more disturbing, a couple have phoned (one sober on a Saturday afternoon, another drunk at 2:00 A.M. one weeknight) offering that I should not say anything about any of these waters because others will be led to them and the fishing will suffer. Both called me a "whore."

Sensitive by nature, rarely angered, always patient, eager to listen and help out, I gave both individuals the benefit of my limited experience and offered direct suggestions about what they could do with their telephones during slack periods of their lives, which I suspect are most of the time.

Their complaints did strike a receptive chord in me, though. Like most of us, my favorite waters are entities that I wish could remain pristine and for me alone to fish. Years ago I thought that keeping "the big secret" would protect my favorite places from the thundering herd.

I was, oh, so wrong. The East Fork of the Yaak is finished from clear-cutting. Some small, delightful brooks in the Bitterroot are lost to developers. The Boulder River near Big Timber and the Ruby are privatized by and for the self-appointed elite. The Jefferson and Big Hole are hammered yearly by gluttonous agrarian water demands. On and on it goes, and to put things bluntly into perspective, the situation is *bullshit!*

The days of hoarding and holding little treasures for myself are unfortunately all but over. And that, too, is what this book is about. I'd much rather share a stream with someone wielding a fly rod than with some crazed clown diverting water by gouging a streambed with a D-9 or destroying a riparian corridor with a chain saw. The only way to save what we still have left to fish is to educate those who have not chosen our addictive way, and to band together. I suppose this is B.S. also, but a trout stream or a sweet lake can die a wicked death in one season at the hands of the ruthless modifiers.

As Wayne Hadley of the Montana Department of Fish, Wildlife and Parks said, "John, we're at the point where we just can't afford to lose any more trout habitat. We just don't have any more to waste."

Wayne is on the mark as always, and that is one of the compelling reasons for runnin' down the blues on the Middle Fork of the Flathead, the Swan, Blackfoot, Jefferson, the Tongue, and the Sun. They're all threatened one way or another, and I love them all and want to see them remain the rivers they are today. They are all a blast to fish and observe and spend time with. Each has a mind of its own as it flows through wildly different land, from the forested mystery on the Middle Fork to the coulee-and-bluff starkness of the Tongue and everything in between. Good country, all of it.

Montana is under siege, big time.

So call me a whore. I sure wish someone had called me that concerning a story I should have written (but unfortunately never did) about the East Fork of the Yaak years ago, when the drainage still had trees. Calling a writer names often means he's doing something right and good (we all trip up once in a while), and maybe if I'd done the right thing there would still be twenty-four-inch trout in the little thing. Save the obscene phone calls for the ones doing the real damage. Enjoying a river is fine, but send a little of the buzz back. Give the developers and the clear-cutters and the rest of the malignant cabal some heat. Make the cost of doing business as usual uncomfortable and costly. Things are so desperate way out here in my bloodshot eyes that I can even see some value in Earth First!

Jive. Jive. Jive. All the time jive. What happened to the little-kid days with a can of worms and a True Temper pole and a creek filled with Red Horse?

They are dead and gone and we're not little kids anymore. The joys of self-justification and bountiful righteousness have swelled my breast: I think I'll head over to the upper end of Whitefish Lake and make obscene gestures into the surveillance cameras guarding the privacy of a newly moved in TV personality. And, what the hell, I'm feelin' more than alright. Let's take down the "No Trespassing" signs her neighbor has put up next to the bridge crossing Swift Creek. And maybe after that I'll go up the road and take on that road grader. Boy, I bet that sucker would make a racket rolling down the mountain. And then . . .

"John?"

"Yes."

"Someone is here to take you fishing."

"Oh? Okay . . . should I take the 4-weight?"

"If you think it's best, John."

"Thanks, Lynda. I'll be back in a little bit."

"We're all hoping . . ."

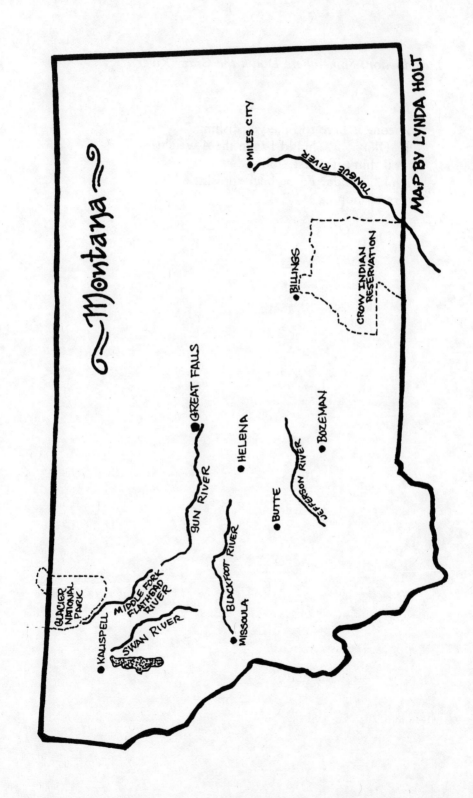

*Montana*

MILES CITY

TONGUE RIVER

MAP BY LYNDA HOLT

BILLINGS

CROW INDIAN RESERVATION

GREAT FALLS

BOZEMAN

HELENA

SUN RIVER

JEFFERSON RIVER

BUTTE

BLACKFOOT RIVER

MIDDLE FORK FLATHEAD RIVER

GLACIER NATIONAL PARK

MISSOULA

SWAN RIVER

KALISPELL

# MIDDLE FORK
## *of the*
# FLATHEAD RIVER

*A*fter about four hundred nine-inch cutthroat trout, most people would call a halt to the proceedings. How many fish does a person need to catch and release, especially this eager, unsophisticated, downscale variety? My friend and I were not ones to stop for anything as long as there was water to float and some action left in our arms. Rugged trout-hunting fly fishers at the peak of their predatory powers wallowing along through the heart of a gorgeous late-July afternoon on the Middle Fork of the Flathead River.

A ninety-degrees breeze cruised over the surface of the clear water that flashed sapphire overtones. The chipped and blasted peaks of Glacier National Park shimmered in the heat behind us on the eastern horizon. There were some cumulus clouds riding the airwaves, but we were not taking them seriously. They'd be nothing but dissipated moisture long gone in a clear night sky within hours.

The river moved with enough zip most of the time to keep the float fast-paced and interesting. Not the Class V madness of spring runoff that draws world-champion local kayaking whackos in small lemminglike hordes each spring to bob and dip and smash and crash in the icy chocolate brown torrent, but swift enough for our pedestrian appetites.

A 4-weight with a nine-foot leader tapered to 5X and an Elk Hair Caddis, something in a #14, please, did the trick. Forty-foot casts along current seams next to midstream boulders and through bankside runs turned fish all of the time. Silvery little cutts would

*The Middle Fork of the Flathead below West Glacier.*

rise at the first sight of the fly and porpoise madly as the furry imitation swung rapidly in the current at the end of a drift. Like all river trout, they fought well if their small size was factored into the struggle.

"Nice cast, John. You make that four land on the water just like an eight," my friend comments as I quickly slap a pile of slack line back into a run where I missed a willing trout.

"Thanks. Might as well see what this thing can handle."

"If it lasts the day it's one hell of a rod."

"You bet."

A few cutthroat and a rainbow or two up to fifteen inches were also taken, but the little ones outnumbered the lunkers by ten to one. The heat and searing sunlight were keeping the larger cutthroat, rainbows, and hybrids of the two species down deep. There are not a lot of big fish in the Middle Fork. The system is on the glacier-melt, sterile side of life, but every now and then a twenty-inch trout makes a mistake, especially when a Woolly Bugger or garish Girdle Bug tumbles down through a deep fast run, to keep you alert, expectant.

The Middle Fork comes into being in the Bob Marshall Wilderness fifty or so air miles from our present location below West Glacier. Around Gooseberry Park, Clack, Bowl, Trail, and Strawberry creeks — all lovely little mountain wilderness streams filled with native westslope cutthroat and big migratory bull trout — come together and the main river takes on a life of its own. This is uncut, unspoiled forest that gives way to severe cliffs and peaks of ancient rock. A part of the nation's Wild and Scenic River System, the Middle Fork flows from the Bob Marshall Wilderness (unfortunately referred to by those with feigned familiarity with this rugged land as "The Bob") into the Great Bear Wilderness before forming the southern boundary of Glacier Park at its confluence with Bear Creek, next to U.S. 2 just east of Java. The river glides through thick forests of aspen, larch, fir, and lodgepole, often squeezing between steep walls of purple-slate rock.

Running, tumbling, falling, and dancing through some of the best country left in the West, the Middle Fork does not rank high on anyone's list of trophy trout waters. There are some good fish here to be sure, including the big bulls that run upriver to secret spawning grounds beginning in the spring. But the low nutrient level of the water, resulting from the drainage cutting through hard rock and deriving meager sustenance from glacial flour, forest detritus, and, increasingly, man-generated nonpoint pollution sources, does not provide enough food for an abundant insect community. There are several species of stoneflies and caddisflies along with an assortment of mayflies and midges, but it is slim pickings in the best of times, especially when compared to rivers like the Missouri or Madison.

For me the main attraction of the Middle Fork is its remote character, even where it rips alongside Highway 2. Pickups, campers, and various models of passenger cars whiz by as I fish the deep blue runs and holes, but a little walking away from the road over logjams and stumbling along the uneven boulder bars takes me to another world. Casting, working the drift, and looking way into the mountains at the head of Muir Creek across-stream in Glacier is all it takes to shift into wilderness illusion. Mount Saint Nicholas stabs at the sky with as much visual force as the Matterhorn. There is bear scat along the shore. Whitetails browse in the timber on the other side of the Middle Fork. A water ouzel bobs in the fast water near me. Trout caught here are a welcome bonus but really only an excuse to be out standing in the river feeling it push against my legs.

And the concentration that is so much a part of serious fishing completes the transformation from highway traveler to lone citizen of the planet. I just don't hear the traffic when I'm in the water.

A couple of rafting companies located near the tourist town of West Glacier turn a good dollar floating swells down the river, but there are few fly fishers who seem to give a damn about this water, except for some that float the wilderness stretches.

From Java down to the confluence with the North Fork at Blankenship Bridge, northwest of Columbia Falls, the only people you'll see working the Middle Fork, outside of my friend and me and a few other optimistic souls, are spin and bait fishers. You'll spot them perched on flat rocks dredging worms, maggots, corn, or deer hindquarters in the deep pools. Six-packs of beer are never very far away, unlike our spartanly provisioned raft that contains two sun-baked fly fishers, five fly rods, ten thousand flies ranging from #22 Blue-Winged Olives to 2/0 pike flies, floatant, and coolers filled with water, beer, soda, sandwiches, bags of sunflower seeds, and a couple types of homemade bread. There are also two packs of stale Camels for health purposes. The things are so dry they ignite like exploding cigars at the touch of a match. High sport, and they taste good, too. Cameras, fishing vests, sunglasses, and raingear are also packed under the seats. We planned to be on the water for upwards of six hours, so this was well-honed, austere existence at its refined and riverine best.

Aside from casting to the cutthroat and rainbows with drys, what used to draw attention were bull trout as they moved up out of Flathead Lake, located a few miles south of Kalispell, and into the three forks of the Flathead—Middle, North, and South, though the South Fork run is virtually nonexistent since the completion in the fifties of Hungry Horse Dam, several miles upstream.

Unfortunately for me and especially for the bull trout, a drastic drop in their numbers forced the Montana Department of Fish, Wildlife and Parks to vote for an indefinite suspension of all fishing for the species west of the Continental Divide. The closure will remain in force until bull trout redds return to documented average levels for two successive years. This is somewhere far off in the undefined future, so for now all fly fishers can do is drift back to outings past and hope the fish recovers soon.

The fish moving up the North Fork are possibly greater in number and size than are their Middle Fork cousins, but some of the bull trout make truly impressive trips into tiny out-of-the-way tributaries in the Bob Marshall Wilderness complex. Fish of several pounds or more have been caught in small streams bubbling into the river's headwaters, which are not exactly roaring flows themselves. And big bull trout have been documented running up Bear Creek, a stream you can easily walk or even jump across in its upper reaches below Marias Pass. These large trout then wriggle and squirm under the safety of darkness into even smaller streams to pair up and spawn in the clean water and gravel of the high country.

The bulls, along with the cutthroat, were easily caught in the headwaters. The fish are wild and took streamers and even drys with almost monotonous consistency. By the time the bull trout had reached this part of the drainage they were pretty well played out from the run and ready for spawning. Catching one, playing it swiftly and fairly, then carefully releasing it never bothered me. Taking more than one fish stirred my conscience. Connecting with one was like touching what was untamed and unspoiled, a good and increasingly necessary experience in this boogie-electric age, and understandable behavior for curious fly fishers. Any more than one and the situation would have approached selfishness. Whatever. The decision is moot for now.

Heading up along Bear Creek, the main northern east-west route of Burlington Northern parallels U.S. 2, both keeping steady company with the stream. Huge snowsheds constructed of large, sturdy timbers protect the tracks from the tons of heavy snow that pour down the steep slopes in deadly speeds and with such vehemence that they create their own brief but intense windstorms. The road, especially around Marias Pass, is often closed by these events or from raging snowstorms. This is one stretch of highway I avoid whenever possible in the winter. You can die on this road in a heartbeat in the cold months.

Some years back a train derailed near here, spilling tons of corn that was never completely cleaned up. The stuff did a wild version of the fermentation two-step and was for a time considered one of the better Rocky Mountain nighttime hangouts by discerning Northern Continental Divide Ecosystem grizzlies. The big bears filled up their stomachs with the protein-rich grain and got pretty well stoned in the process. You used to be able to drive to the place in the dark and watch the bears have a good time, but government authorities in all their wisdom decided everyone was enjoying themselves a little too much and placed this activity out of bounds. The corn has been cleaned up and the scene of the crime buried under several feet of soil and boulders.

The point of all this is that even near a major rail line and highway, Middle Fork country is wild, good land. There are the bears and fish and eagles and elk and goats and good forest.

The trees, though, are constantly threatened by the unquenchable thirst of the timber industry. Cuts in the Challenge and Dodge Creek areas up Bear Creek led to massive slumping of fragile soils during periods of runoff and heavy rains. The sediment washed into the streams and buried prime bull trout spawning gravels in choking muck. The fish are extremely selective when it comes to sites for building redds. The Flathead drainage is slowly choking in sediment pouring into bull trout spawning areas; this is due mainly to excessive logging, much of it in dwindling stands of old growth.

Montana Department of Fish, Wildlife and Parks surveys indicate that bull trout redd numbers have been declining steadily for the past few years. That is why the agency closed the season and is actively working on other measures to restore the fishery. Admittedly, there are some meat-hunting slobs taking large numbers of the species. But blaming anglers for the decline of the bull trout while the timber industry continues to devastate the region's forests seems inappropriate.

And this inappropriateness may reach even higher levels. Instead of placing habitat preservation and restoration at the top of the bull trout recovery list, a strong sentiment has surfaced that wants to augment wild trout with hatchery-raised fish.

One of the major attractions of fly fishing is the myth and lore dealing with casting over and fighting wild, native trout in pristine waters. Images of riotously colored fish flying through the air or crashing downstream in valiant efforts at escape and freedom are part of our elaborate pursuit. With bull trout (and westslope cutthroat trout) habitat destruction increasing at an insane pace from the avaricious attentions of the usual suspects, which mainly include logging, oil and gas exploration, and residential development interests, the stress on prime trout water is growing at an explosive rate. At the same time, anglers demand more than the status quo regarding current levels of catchable trout populations and clamor for still greater numbers of fish to satisfy febrile trout-fishing dreams.

There are only so many wild native trout in Montana, and the number of waters that can support these wonderful specimens is steadily declining. State fish and game personnel are feeling the intense pressure to satisfy our need for a quality fishing experience. They are often responding with a quick fix of hatchery trout as opposed to the more time-consuming and costly solution of habitat improvement and restoration.

Public bureaucracies by their very nature are readily susceptible to the often ill-informed whims of public opinion and desire, frequently in direct opposition to their own management beliefs, which are usually supported by loads of data and years of experience. Does an infusion of hatchery fish (dubbed "rubber trout" by author Robert H. Smith in *Native Trout of North America*) introduce a weakened gene pool to wild fish populations that gradually saps the feral characteristics from the native species? Do stocked fish displace wild trout? Is this form of trout management the wave of the future or a behavior that needs to be swatted on its hindquarters by the rolled newspaper of public concern whenever it begins to squat near our vanishing store of unspoiled lakes and streams?

A number of government agencies and private entities are involved in this mess, including the Montana Department of Fish, Wildlife and Parks, the U.S. Fish and Wildlife Service, the Confederated Salish and Kootenai Tribes, and area anglers. The problems and disparate opinions surfacing in this region serve as a good example of things to come for many watersheds in the rest of the country, and the West in particular.

At the center of the controversy is a proposal to spend $400,000 to build bull trout rearing facilities. The money comes from a federal fund designated to mitigate the impact on the Flathead River fishery by operation of the Hungry Horse Dam. The dam has blocked upstream migrations of both bull and westslope cutthroat trout. Power generating regimes have disrupted normal flows and released unnatural amounts of cold water.

This sizable allocation for hatchery stock would cut into money earmarked for bull trout habitat restoration. The plan calls for releasing as many as 250,000 hatchery-reared bull trout into Flathead Lake. This caused one Montana Department of Fish, Wildlife and Parks fisheries biologist to express some concern.

"I was worried about the possibility of genetic variability loss if we relied too heavily on hatchery fish, which could overwhelm natural populations of bull trout," said Tom Weaver of the FWP. "I expressed views that we should proceed slowly, on a truly experimental basis, with hatchery fish and also that we should be doing more to restore habitat. I was worried initially, but I am pretty pleased with the way they listened and the way things are going now."

"They" is a trio of biologists from the FWP, the U.S. Fish and Wildlife Service, and the Federated Salish and Kootenai Tribes, whose reservation is located along the southern end of Flathead Lake along the Mission Mountains.

"There are valid concerns here, and we don't want to screw up," commented Joe DosSantos, who represented the tribes on the team. "We've done nothing yet. Everything is on paper. There is now a biologist at FWP that will work full-time studying the situation. His input will be used to prepare a supplementation plan for the species. We will also be talking with geneticists outside of the state to help find out if this is doable."

Bull trout are extremely susceptible to changes in their environment. Logging, development, and road-building all threaten the fish's existence. Because of this sensitivity, bull trout are listed as "indicator species" in the Flathead National Forest Plan. In other words, what is bad for the bull trout is more than likely bad for the rest of the environment.

The total catch for bull trout in the Flathead drainage was only a few thousand fish per year, an obvious indication that numbers for the species are not all that high and probably were never prolific historically. Even in the best of times bull trout experience a fragile, precarious existence, a factor the planning team must take into account when they devise a management program.

In addition, this concern is now manifesting itself in the form of the lower numbers of bull trout redds. Redds are used by biologists as a measuring stick for fish populations. And a number of fisheries biologists and geneticists outside of the various agencies involved here also expressed concern about a massive stocking program.

As more and more information becomes available about genetic qualities that have allowed salmonids to adapt to certain watersheds, the question increasingly posed is: Are populations of fish for specific drainages actually definable subspecies? The concern here is whether or not populations of native salmonids have evolved and adapted to a unique set of river or stream variables, a process that allows these fish not only to survive but even to flourish in their home waters. And because of this, would the swamping of these native populations with hatchery fish containing traits from other drainages prove catastrophic?

Definitely a complicated question.

"I think the plan is too strong on hatcheries, too ambitious," said Rob Leary of the University of Montana genetics lab in Missoula. "We don't know anything about the population's genetic structure in the system. There could be a bunch of differing genetic groups that sort themselves out in the spawning run."

Flathead River bull trout hold in Flathead Lake during the winter before heading up the three main forks of the river and then farther still up into wild, isolated mountain streams before spawning. The run to these remote waters can cover over one hundred miles. Most of the survivors eventually return downstream to Flathead Lake to regroup before another run.

While bull trout have their own unique set of variables, their situation in northwest Montana may also serve as a strong example of what could or is happening to other native salmonid populations in the West. Perhaps stocking cutthroat in the Snake River system is destroying key gene traits that make that river's trout beautiful and unique. Or hatchery programs in Oregon and Washington could be destroying large numbers of native trout. Indeed, the Madison River is thriving as a wild trout fishery due mainly to the state's decision to stop planting hatchery trout. The river withstands tremendous fishing pressure and for the most part the trout are in good shape.

"What's needed is a two- or three-year study to figure out what diversity is present," adds Leary. "There may be a lot of genetic groups up there and a large plant of hatchery fish could swamp the wild gene pool. On the other hand, I could envision taking cutthroat and bull trout from nearby streams to plant in an adjacent creek that needs to be helped along. Highly domesticated fish might not be able to compete, but wild eggs may be a different story."

The plan appears to address at least some of Leary's concerns. There will be a FWP biologist studying the situation on a full-time basis. Eggs used for fry production will be taken from the wild each year for imprint plantings.

"Bulls do not like people, that's pretty straightforward," says Joe DosSantos. "And there is no arguing that habitat destruction and the effects of the recent droughts have harmed the population. We need to preserve and restore habitat. No question there. We haven't allowed fishing for bull trout on our land [the reservation] for some time now.

"But another point to consider is that bull trout are now in Category 2 as defined by the Endangered Species Act. This means they are close to Category 1, or Officially Threatened or Endangered. If they become listed (as is now being considered) the U.S. Fish and Wildlife Service will take over and take the species into the hatchery system.

"This is a contentious issue. We want to do things right, but we also have a lot to be learning here."

"They are under the gun up there ever since the [Flathead Lake] fishery collapsed," says Robert Behnke, a world-renowned authority on trout and a professor in the Department of Fishery and Wildlife Biology at Colorado State University in Fort Collins. "The factors that caused the problem cannot be reversed. The introduction of the mysis shrimp is responsible for this decline of the bull trout, cutthroat, and kokanee, and the boom in the lake trout and lake whitefish populations."

Behnke is referring to the introduction of mysis shrimp into lakes upstream of Flathead Lake in the early eighties. The thought was

that the mysis would provide an ideal food source for the kokanee
salmon that were attracting the attentions of meat fishers and also
hundreds of bald eagles along McDonald Creek during the fall
spawning run. Quite a sight in its heyday. Unfortunately, the
shrimp outcompeted with the salmon for the fish's primary food
source — zooplankton — and the salmon population collapsed.

Since this disaster (in the eyes of some), Flathead Lake has been
a sea of chaos. Lake Superior whitefish compose eighty percent
of its biomass. Lake trout are now found as far north as British
Columbia in the North Fork. Many biologists and fly fishers fear
that the lake trout are greatly reducing bull trout numbers through
predation. The lake trout are aided in their takeover by cold-water
discharges from Hungry Horse Dam during power generation.
A mitigation plan that proposes drawing warmer water from
higher in the reservoir's water column may push the species back
down below the mouths of the Middle and North forks. Only
time will tell.

Robert Behnke continues: "Why do they think that hatchery
fish will do any better? I critiqued the program up there and I
don't think they will have much success with hatchery fish. They
are not very capable of surviving on their own in the wild.

"Survival will probably be so poor that there may not be much
of a genetics problem. My main concern would be with the possible transmission of diseases often found in hatcheries. This could
be much more serious."

Another reason this is an issue in the first place is the habitat
destruction that has been occurring for years in the forested mountains of this corner of Montana. At an ever-increasing pace,
riparian habitat along key spawning and rearing streams has disappeared as forests are logged and developers madly rush in to
make a quick buck on the public's desire to live in the woods.
A loss of habitat equals a loss in bull trout (and other wild species)
numbers.

Logging roads and clear-cuts need to be replanted with indigenous species of trees. Riparian areas need to be restored and silt
must be flushed from key portions of prime streams. Developers

need to be reined in (if not regulated out of existence). Replace the lost miles of quality stream-course and the numbers of large wild trout will return. The problem here is that habitat restoration is more expensive than hatchery programs, at least in the short run. Benefits from trout plantings appear immediately; fixing a damaged stream may not yield results for years. Much of the fishing public wants to catch trout *right now!*

Until this healing process gets underway with serious intent, the issue of wild versus hatchery trout will be with us.

Whitefish fly fisher and active Trout Unlimited member Mike Brennan speaks for many when he says with some vehemence: "Natural is better. A natural fish is wilier. Fishing for wild trout, for a fish that has been here forever, is a state of mind. A matter of aesthetics. Casting to hatchery fish . . . you may as well be at Billy Bob's Trout Farm as far as I'm concerned."

Testify, Brother! And thankfully working a small dry on the Middle Fork is still a pretty wild experience in all senses of the word.

While the bug life in and around the river (with the exception of some aggressive mosquitoes) is a touch on the slim side, there are enough insects to warrant at least cursory attention by the angler.

The salmonfly and related stonefly hatches found in late spring along rivers like the Big Hole, the Madison, and Rock Creek are justly famous. On the Middle Fork, several species of Plecoptera make sometimes significant appearances.

Frequently when floating the river we pull over for fish runs that have either proven themselves on past outings or that look promising. The river gradually drops in flow as the season progresses (amazing how things work in nature), and in each instance of wading we, usually my friend Mike Brennan and I, have spotted good numbers of stonefly exoskeletons on rocks just above the current water level. This would seem to indicate that one species or another is hatching at various times of day throughout the months of March through at least October. We've often seen large specimens lumbering skyward during our floats but have never observed a true hatch even approaching salmonfly dimensions. Maybe there are none of this intensity on the river.

Among the more "significant" stoneflies are *Pteronarcys badia,* similar to *californica* but smaller, occurring in late July above West Glacier; skwala species in late April; members of the Chloroperlidae clan, flying around from summer into autumn, that are easily imitated with Elk Hair Caddis from #12–16; and fair numbers of Perlodidae from midsummer into fall, imitated by Sofa Pillows, caddis ties, and a Golden Stone, all from #4–8. Obviously, the nymph stages on 3X and 4X hooks take fish normally larger on average than those fooled with drys, but surface work is more fun than nymphing in most instances.

One of the more curious stonefly groups includes *Paaraperla frontalis, Isocapnia missouri, I. crinita,* and *I. grandis.* Biologists have collected these species just prior to emergence on the Flathead River but have not been able to find any earlier instars, fueling speculation that these stoneflies experience early development in the groundwater.

This was confirmed when residents of Eureka, fifty miles to the north of Whitefish, began finding nymphs in their tap water. The source of the stoneflies was a new municipal water system that drew from the floodplain aquifer, which was 15 feet deep and up to 165 feet inland from the Tobacco River shoreline just west of the Flathead River basin. Municipal pumps were drawing both water and three-quarter-inch stonefly nymphs from saturated underground gravels. Filtration solved the problem, but further study revealed an elaborate community containing midges, beetles, leeches, and early instars of mayflies and other stoneflies.

These creatures live off organic detritus and algae along with other invertebrates. Spaces in the loosely compacted floodplain gravels are large enough to let the insects move about freely. One wonders what else is living beneath the surface of our awareness.

*Baetis* and even *Callibaetis* become evident by the time the days begin cooling in late August and are productive for some time into September. Blue-Winged Olives from #18–20 work reasonably well on overcast days. Ameletus appear about the same time, gradually dwindling into late October. Nymphs in brown tones on 3XL hooks work best, especially when weighted. Reddish gray duns and spinners also produce. Members of the *Ephemerella* genus start appearing noticeably in late June, peaking in August and gradually fading through September. Patterns running the gamut from Green Drakes early on through PMDs cover this action, with nymphs producing the best in the calmer runs of the river. *Heptagenia* matched with a Light Cahill in #12–16 also interest the fish.

Caddis are represented best by *Rhyacophila, Hydropsyche, Brachycentrus,* and, significantly in the fall on the main river and the tributaries, members of Limnephilidae known as fall caddis. Soft hackles worked with a slight touch of upward twitch on an otherwise dead drift always take fish, even bull trout on occasion. I carry a box of Elk Hair Caddis (easily one of the best of the many fine patterns designed and/or refined by Al Troth) tied in #12–18 in shades from tan to nearly black, with an assortment of fall caddis in #12–16 tied tan with an orange chenille body. These really work and have turned the biggest cutthroat (twenty-three inches) and rainbows I've seen on the Middle Fork. This version also produces on Rock Creek and, early in the season, on most of the freestone mountain streams in my part of the state. The body color probably imitates some smaller stoneflies and possibly has attractor characteristics as well.

There are also larger numbers of grasshoppers beginning as early as late May. From midday on they create a steady, almost subliminal background of clacking as they leap and briefly soar among the rocks and bushes. I find that large light-colored Elk Hair Caddis (#8–12) cover this action, but Brennan in his never-ending quest to push the fly-tying-reality envelope to its utter extremes prefers a hopper tie that can only be called "awfully damn big," but it works. He also has a pattern he calls the Ugly Bitch that is something of a Bitch Creek with peacock herl for a body coupled with other garish attachments. Drifting this fly down into deep runs and pools, Brennan connects with some good rainbows.

The fly seems to outproduce the Bugger, at least in northwest Montana.

Attractor patterns like Royal Humpies and Wulffs also produce, as do Woolly Buggers and other streamers.

The bottom line for me is the Elk Hair Caddis, a long-bodied nymph and something like the Ugly Bitch. The fish are not sophisticated or pressured, and average on a good day just on the short side of a foot.

Important food sources for cutthroat (and to a lesser extent rainbows and hybrids) in the river in order of relative importance are caddis, mayflies, dipterans, stoneflies, ants-bees-wasps, beetles, and even spiders. The order of preference for families of mayflies is Ephemerellidae, Baetidae, and Heptageniidae. For caddis, the list is Limnephilidae, Rhyacophilidae, Hydropsychidae, and Brachycentridae. Bull trout prefer — when not eating other fish — mayflies, stoneflies, true flies, then caddis. The same holds pretty much true for the non-native brook trout holding the tributaries. Many of these little flows appear on maps but are often too small, too much studded with natural migrational barriers, or too brushy to bother fishing, unless you are into nonproductive masochism.

But enough of this turgid silliness. To quote a reporter friend of mine, who always grumbled at the end of an unusually tough day on the job, "That's enough of that. Holt, let's get a drink." Amazing how many tough days there were back there in southern Wisconsin covering murders, tornadoes, lousy prep football games, and liquor-store stickups.

Whether floating or wading along the Middle Fork, ignoring the geology of the region is nearly impossible. Looking south into the primitive pine forests that flow deep green toward barren ridges of rock and ice, or north up narrow drainages to the wild alpine country of Glacier, the land's ancient origins are everywhere.

If you take a few hours and drive U.S. 2 from Columbia Falls to East Glacier, you will cross the Northern Montana Overthrust Belt. Most of Glacier Park is a huge slab, two miles thick, of Precambrian belt rocks that slid east thirty-five miles or more. The rocks are more than a billion years old and rest on top of Cretaceous

*October: The Middle Fork up near Java with a view into Glacier Park.*

sedimentary rocks that check in at a youthful 65 to 100 million years. This formation lies on top of Paleozoic rocks that contain the first animal fossils—ancient stuff. The Precambrian rocks moved along the surface of the Lewis Overthrust Belt, an event my mind cannot visualize even when looking east into the park from the nearby Whitefish Range. The idea of that entire mass of towering, twisted rock sliding several dozen miles east is too much for my easily addled brain.

Nonetheless, the rocks you will see along the highway from Columbia Falls to the top of Marias Pass are the same Precambrian sedimentary formations as those found on the west side of the park along the North Fork. Gazing north into the mountains of Glacier at windy Marias Pass you can see the fault angling slightly eastward, and in a few spots black Cretaceous shale is visible. Rock above the Lewis Overthrust is Precambrian, and that below the belt is sedimentary and accumulated in and near a shallow inland sea around 80 million years ago.

Small fossil ammonites appear in the shale. They look like large snails but are more likely octopuslike creatures that lived in a shell. These animals flourished in the sea but disappeared in the same catastrophic event that did a number on the dinosaurs.

The Middle Fork Valley was filled with ice coming down from the mountains on both sides in the last ice age. This glacier scoured its way down to an even larger glacier in the Flathead Valley. The ice was six thousand feet deep at the Canadian border but thinned quickly, ending just south of Flathead Lake. Eastward-retreating glaciers left numerous small moraines, and at one time a sheet of deep ice extended out onto the high plains east of Browning.

Aside from the spectacular visuals offered by all of this dramatic and massive activity, the influence on the dynamics of the Middle Fork as a trout stream are important. Tremendous amounts of runoff from spring rains and snowmelt scour the tributary and main river stream-courses, an annual situation that is largely responsible for the marginal insect communities in the Middle Fork system. Life is tough if you are a bug in this water. Nutrient levels are low because of the steep, relatively young nature of the valley. (Look at the mineral-rich surroundings of rivers like the Bighorn or Missouri. The country is older and the land alongside the streams is more sedate and stable.) Even if insects can eke out an existence in this water, the spring torrents often wash them away downstream. This lack of invertebrates definitely places limits and sets average size and numbers on the trout in the river.

The lack of fertility in the river is readily apparent when I hike into the Great Bear Wilderness portion of the Bob Marshall complex. Heading upriver from its junction with Bear Creek, the trail crosses dry streambeds, ephemeral flows that are barely trickles on this particular July day, and before I come to Spruce Creek, which drops precipitously down to the narrow canyon, the Middle Fork rips through just inside the Wilderness. Hiking down to the river is exciting as I slip and slide along a six-inch-wide game trail just across from Dirty Face Creek. Deer and elk pellets mark the trail. A wrong step would mean a head-over-heels tumble ending in many broken bones or death, but so what — trout are in the offing.

Down along the sand-and-boulder beach that lines the east side of the river, the remains of an old cabin or shack are decomposing into the ground. Another year's runoff should complete the process. Forested slopes block the sky in the west. The sun is hot as always when I'm hiking, and the Middle Fork runs like ice-cold emeralds over rock shaded rust, pink, and gray. Long glides, extended rapids, and pools over twenty feet deep mark this mile-and-one-half stretch of water.

Casting a large Sofa Pillow to imitate the usually sparse hatch of golden stones that have only recently moved farther upstream into the wilderness draws the attention of a couple of ten-inch cutthroat but nothing else. The pattern looks marvelous riding high on the river's surface, but the jaunty appearance does little for the bigger fish.

I switch to Polly Rosborough's Golden Stone for a better match, and a twelve-inch cutthroat takes immediately, then a fourteen-inch fish, and then another. The pattern produces up and down the stretch, even drawing the trout from deep in the clear pools. They come slowly but deliberately to the surface, first a light shadow that gradually takes shape and then definition before, mouths agape, the fish come down on the pattern. As soon as they feel the hook they thrash and splash along the surface, the spray quicksilvery in the light.

This is what the walk was for: native trout in wild surroundings. I'm alone and at ease. The trout never exceed that magic fourteen-inch barrier, but length is not important. For what is scorned by most for being a small-trout fishery, the Middle Fork does all right in my eyes.

Working back to the log where my gear is stowed in the shade, I connect with a couple more trout, smaller, maybe ten inches, but beautiful, sparkling things. I grab a can of beer that was chilling in a little eddy of the river, pop the lid, and drink slowly, foam running down my chin and onto my shirt. Some sharp Cheddar and a bunch of red grapes complete the feast, and I lie down in the sand with the log as a backrest. Lying here alone in the soft silence of the river I wonder what the land was like in the 1840s, when the Middle Fork was named Riviere de Smet after an early missionary, Father Jean Pierre DeSmet.

And the myth concerning the name Flathead drifts by. Someone long ago named Shining Shirt led his "mystery people" out of the distant west. They were neither white nor Indian, but claimed that they or their fathers had come from beyond the sea in a large boat that foundered near shore. They married coastal women but eventually wandered inland and began living with the Kalispels on Flathead Lake. These travelers taught the Salish (still present today on the Flathead Indian Reservation) many new things, including more efficient ways to build fires and better medicine. They were eventually absorbed into the Salish. Though none of the Salish flattened the heads of their babies in cradleboards, contrary to popular folklore, some of the coastal people who came with Shining Shirt did. Some research suggests that Shining Shirt and his people may have been sailors from Spanish galleons shipwrecked at the mouth of the Columbia River. The shining shirt may well have been mail or armor.

On rare occasions, the true sense or feel of times past is overpowering. The Flathead country has this effect on me with greater frequency the longer I live here. The Shining Shirt myth is one of the most compelling: the notion of the sailors struggling over mountains and across the eastern Washington desert to reach the Flathead, a land that radiated all the trappings of Paradise, I'm sure.

Too much thought, advancing senility no doubt, and sleep glides over me like a soft push away from the real world. Cooler air sifting down through the trees as the sun loses intensity while closing in on the high horizon nudges me awake. I stumble around, not quite sure of my identity (a common event), break down the rod, and start up the trail.

A sweet day in fine country with willing fish.

You could spend a summer working your way up and then back down the Middle Fork in the wilderness, and maybe I'll do that sometime.

I've always wanted to fish the streams pouring out of Glacier to the north, but they are closed to protect spawning bull trout,

and there are plenty of bears there, too. Park bears are unpre-
dictable, and I avoid most of Glacier's backcountry. Grizzlies make
northwest Montana the high-energy turf it is, but playing craps
with these bears is a gamble I'm unwilling to take.

Below West Glacier the Middle Fork begins to lose its pristine
character as it flows past homes, resorts, mazes, curio shops, and
bungee-jumping facilities. There are locations where trout can be
taken by a fisherman wading in relative isolation. One such spot,
surrounded by distant mountains, offers about a quarter-mile of
deep runs, swirling seams, and near-shore eddies. The water
borders Glacier, and there are bears nearby. I've seen big blacks
in the woods and splashing across the river upstream. There is
always plenty of fresh scat along the river. A rusting yellow bear
trap baited with a chunk of rotten meat is often positioned in the
woods behind me. Recently a hiker was killed and partially
devoured by a sow grizzly protecting her two cubs only miles from
this spot. Officials killed the bears because they feared the animals
had become "habituated" to human flesh. Three less powerful
magic creatures in the woods these days.

Regardless of these facts, big cutthroat and rainbow stack up
here, feeding on midges, caddis, stoneflies, and grasshoppers,
depending on the season. I don't bother with midges. Working
diminutive larval or pupal imitations in swift water does not
interest me. The drys would be invisible, and the take must be
seen to be worthwhile.

Casting various sizes and shades of Elk Hair Caddis does intrigue me. There is one holding spot along the rocky far shore
that always shelters a couple of trout. Not large, maybe up to
seventeen or eighteen inches, but the cast and the drift are the
challenge.

The distance is sixty feet, and you need to throw in a downstream reach and make a couple of quick mends in the middle
of the line to gain a drift of a dozen feet or so—one that is long
enough to interest the fish and give them time to take. Complicat-
ing the situation is the fact that an upstream wind is almost always
blowing by prime fishing time in the afternoon. This requires that

you throw in something bordering on a double-reach to compensate for the wind pushing the belly of the line upstream.

I've fished this little spot often and can now successfully complete the maneuver more than half the time. Once done, the line needs to be constantly, but oh so delicately, stripped in to avoid drag and spooking the trout.

On this late-summer day I shot the line upstream where I wanted it, mended and stripped and watched as two trout rose to the gray caddis. The fish went into the air at the set of the hook, then sounded, running and thrashing at the gravel bottom of the run. I could see its silver sides flash beneath me. The trout held its ground for a moment or two before I was able to force it to shore in ever-tightening circles.

I stepped into the cold water and ran my free hand carefully down the leader to the fly and then gently grasped the fish. I marked it on the rod for later measurement (eighteen inches or a little less). The cutthroat was metallic satin with jet black spotting and orange cuts beneath the jaw. It wriggled from my grasp and shot out of sight. I thought, What the hell? One fish in this country today on this river is plenty.

I walked back to the truck and drove home.

# SWAN RIVER

*I*'d never seen a bull trout jump before. Nor had I ever observed a bull trout with a crimson band running down its flank coupled with hundreds of dark spots scattered across its shoulders, back, and tail. The trout looked to be more than twenty inches, but the markings really were all wrong. Perhaps this was not a member of the *Salvelinus confluentus* contingent, but who's ever heard of a rainbow trout hitting a red-and-white woolhead bendback, especially when dredged through the dark green gut of a swift, deep run in the Swan River? Not this boy.

Friends who enjoy things associated with fly rods had mentioned now and then during informal conversations that rainbows were making a minor comeback of sorts in the river. This big guy at the end of the line might provide proof to these spotty tales. The trout was racehorsing downstream and I staggered back to shore, the smooth pebbles sliding beneath my feet. The fish jumped a couple of times and I followed the action with the rod tip.

This was a big trout by any Montana river standards, and I dearly wanted to hold the thing, to examine the fish closely. The leader was 1X for the bull trout, and the knots were fresh and tight. The hook was sharp, the windshield clean, the tank full of high-test, so I had a shot here. The rod jerked up and down as the rainbow ran downstream and barely into my backing. Then the fish stopped dead in the water, its muscular engine idling sideways to the current. This allowed me to retrieve line by walking down to where he was holding, maintaining line tension, and reeling in the distance between us.

23

I passed the several cans of Pabst I'd left cooling in the river—
a siren call most times, but they'd have to wait. The game was
afoot and a big trout was close at hand.

Coming ever nearer, my silhouette spooked the trout into streak-
ing off again, and line was spinning off the reel in fits and spurts.
The rewind process repeated itself again and then again before
I closed in on the trout, now finning upright in less than six inches
of water. The dusky tan gravels created a flattering background
for the wild thing. Dropping the rod in the water at my feet, I
tailed the trout and then cradled him beneath his belly. This *was*
a nice fish. I marked him along the rod for future measurement.
His appearance was striking—broad crimson band, moss green
back, hooked jaw, and a purplish scar near the dorsal fin that
looked like an attack from a kingfisher that possessed eyes with
power far exceeding that of its lifting capability. I pressed the ten-
second delay on the camera that I had tried to prefocus on the
cheap tripod and posed for a shot, and then a few more. Maybe
they would turn out. Maybe not. Who cared?

The rainbow was still in my hands. He came to slowly in the
calm water, surging back and forth against the resistance of my
grip. With the release he moved off to the far bank, blending into
the river's flickering color scheme and vanishing from my sight.
Many writers extol the joys of turning back a big fish. I suppose
there is that emotion, but the sense of power, the knowledge that
I could have killed the trout but chose to do otherwise, is intoxi-
cating. I mean, how much control do we have over our lives in
this world, anyway? Call this feeling perverted, but also call it
honest. Take what you can get, where you find it. Always.

I pulled a tape from my daypack and measured the length on
the rod—twenty-three inches. A big trout, especially so for the
Swan, which is not noted for large numbers of trout, particularly
rainbows like this one.

After years of claiming twenty-inch fish, I started marking them
against the rod I was using that day. I was not overly surprised
to discover that many (most) of my twenty-inchers were more like
seventeen or eighteen inches. Respectable, but when a trout crosses

that magic twenty-inch line, it becomes a different fish. Compare an eighteen and a twenty and see for yourself. Once they pass twenty-two inches and head for the rarefied atmosphere of two feet, trout become special: trophies, uncommon gifts.

In all my years of fly fishing I've only known one person who underestimates the length of his fish. This soul lives for big trout and takes no pleasure in false estimates. He's the one that swung me over to taping trout. After a few dozen measurements, gauging length becomes routine, for a while at least. Then the much-feared angling-elongation-distortion affliction creeps back into the picture. Out comes the tape again. The size of the fish, like so many things in life, only infrequently has a direct correlation to the level of pleasure experienced by the individual who caught it. Still, knowing the length of one's catch definitely lends dimension to a shaky and variable frame of reference.

Frames of reference boxing in our perceptions and defining the limits of our imaginations. What is the current state of the Swan River trout fishery and what is the potential for this beautiful river that undergoes a constant onslaught of degradations running the ugly range from huge clear-cuts to development to the introduction of non-native species?

If you fish long enough and well enough on the Swan you will eventually catch rainbows, brook trout, mountain whitefish, and westslope cutthroat. You would probably catch a bull trout inadvertently, of course, since the season for these fish is now closed in all streams west of the Continental Divide. In the fall of 1992, several conservation groups asked the U.S. Fish and Wildlife Service to list bull trout as an endangered species, saying that logging and other development have degraded the species habitat. The petition also asked that bull trout receive emergency protection in Idaho, Nevada, Oregon, and Washington. The fish have vanished from at least half of their historic range and are no longer present in California. Montana Department of Fish, Wildlife and Parks (MDFWP) biologists state predation by introduced species like lake trout is probably as much to blame as anything. What is obvious is that the trout are taking a beating at the hands of a

*The beautiful Swan River.*

number of severe threats. Their survival is in doubt. Their loss would be tragic.

From its headwaters in the Mission and Swan mountains, the Swan flows north for approximately sixty-six miles before discharging into Flathead Lake at Bigfork. Fifty-three major tributaries join the river along its course. The drainage covers almost seven hundred square miles, flowing through a densely forested, glaciated valley that is from three to six miles wide. Most of the land is owned by the forest service, Plum Creek Timber Company, and the state of Montana. The immediate river corridor is primarily under private ownership.

Three oligotrophic (high in oxygen and low in nutrients) lakes are part of the system. The southernmost is Lindbergh Lake, 726 acres. Five miles downstream is Holland Lake, 408 acres, and then thirty-five miles farther downstream is Swan Lake, 2,680 acres. The Swan then flows thirteen miles before being impounded by Bigfork Dam, a twelve-foot-high structure built in 1902 and owned by Pacific Power and Light Company. The last mile is basically a whitewater torrent held in high esteem by kayakers around the country. Lindbergh and Holland lakes contain remnant populations of cutthroat and bull trout along with rainbow and kokanee. Swan Lake has good populations of kokanee and bull trout, with low numbers of rainbow and cutthroat and illegally introduced northern pike and lesser game and trash fish. Mysis shrimp have been introduced into Swan Lake, but for some reason have not had the drastic consequences on kokanee numbers that they had in Flathead Lake. Who knows what is going on with the mysis and the salmon?

Research indicates that hatchery planting of undesignated strains of cutthroat may jeopardize pure-strain races, as well as promote further hybridization and suppression of existing populations. During the 1980s, a westslope cutthroat brood stock was developed and has been used to try to rebuild hybridized or lost populations of genetically pure trout.

Based on snorkel and electrofishing surveys, mountain whitefish, rainbow trout, brook trout, then bull trout are the predominant gamefish in the Swan. Westslope cutthroat are present in low numbers but appear to be increasing. Other species surveyed include: longnose sucker, largescale sucker (a personal favorite), northern squawfish, longnose dace, redside shiner, pumpkinseed, sculpin, yellow perch, kokanee, and northern pike.

The river is mainly a fish migration corridor for both bull and remnant numbers of adfluvial cutthroat. Brook trout grow the fastest in the river and have the shortest lifespans. Rainbows are next in growth rate, followed by bull and cutthroat trout.

The upper river below Lindbergh Lake is shallow, with riffles and a few small pools and a flow averaging 165 cfs. Rainbow and brooks predominate and run less than twelve inches. Few other trout are present. The middle stretch of the Swan has increased flows, better channel diversity, and large, deep pools developed from piles of logs and other debris blocking the river. There may be as many as one hundred rainbow trout over twelve inches per mile here. Brook trout, though smaller, number around

350 fish per mile. Whitefish come in at over one thousand per mile, and there are fair numbers of cutthroat also. The lower stretch above Swan Lake has the greatest habitat diversity and a flow of about 1,000 cfs. Rainbows are the most numerous of the trout, with as many as 150 over twelve inches per mile, followed in order by brook and bull trout. Whitefish clocked in at nearly fifteen hundred per mile. Cutthroat are also present. Below Swan Lake, fish run larger but are greatly reduced in number due to increased amounts of silt and higher water temperatures. The final, mad mile holds rainbow and cutthroat, along with bull and lake trout and lake and mountain whitefish.

Cutthroat occupy a special place in my heart. They are beautiful. They are wild and they swim in streams flowing through the remains of some of the best country anywhere. A love of good country goes with an addiction to fly fishing. The best part of cutthroat fishing is that prime water is normally situated well away from the mass trappings of the human race. The species takes a lot of heat from many fly fishers who look down their snobbish noses and proclaim that cutthroat are not worth fishing for because they are too easy to catch.

Hey—you clowns won me over with that argument. There's nothing I like better than spending an entire season playing mind games with trout that have seen more flies than René Harrop. Like Ornette Coleman playing the violin, while it's intriguing, a little bit of this action goes a long way. The status of the cutthroat is so precarious that the species' tendency toward eager and aggressive response to even the clumsiest of presentations should be applauded in this age of repressed behavior. Enhancement of their numbers should be among a fly fisher's priorities.

Perhaps ninety-nine percent of the original population of interior cutthroat has disappeared in the last century, certainly a cheerful thought. The name "westslope" led me to believe that the fish were only found on my side of the Continental Divide, but I was wrong. A sizable portion of the trout's original range lies east of the Divide. The present and historical range of the westslope cutthroat includes the upper Missouri River drainage above Fort Benton, as well as the headwaters of the Marias (named by Captain Meriwether Lewis for his cousin and targeted fiancé Maria Wood), Judith, Musselshell, and Milk rivers, which are tributaries that join up with the Missouri below Fort Benton. The subspecies is also found in the South Saskatchewan River system south of the Bow River in the Hudson Bay drainage.

On the west side of the Divide their range includes the Clark Fork drainage above the falls on the Pend Oreille; the Kootenai River drainage from the headwaters to below the confluences of the Moyie and Elk rivers; the Spokane River basin above Spokane Falls, including the Coeur d'Alene and St. Joe river drainages; and the Salmon and Clearwater river drainages. The trout is more than likely the first divergence of an interior cutthroat from the coastal trout. The fish evolved with bull trout and mountain whitefish west of the Divide. Below the barrier falls on the Columbia it lived alongside, though probably not as harmoniously, with a Kamloops strain of rainbow and steelhead and chinook in some Idaho waters. East of the Divide the cutthroat hung out with Arctic grayling and the prolific whitefish.

Westslope cutts probably crossed over the Continental Divide from the west, coming up the Flathead River proper, then the Middle Fork, and finally Bear Creek, arriving in a body of water where some brushy beaver ponds lead to Maria's river via Summit Creek. This happened around seven to ten thousand years ago, or approximately the last time the Chicago Cubs won a World Series.

The Swan runs between the Missions on the West and the Swan Range to the east. Both are impressive structures rising straight up from the valley floor for more than a mile. Rugged cirques hold deep lakes that are often barren or contain small populations of stunted fish. Elk, grizzlies, deer, and the like roam the forested slopes. The rock is Precambrian sedimentary that tilts eastward. Thousands of years ago the Missions split the Bull Lake Ice Age glacier that rumbled down from British Columbia. This split sent a massive tongue down the Swan Valley. Tremendous accumulations of debris in the form of moraines remain today south of Clearwater Junction. When the ice finally retreated to the north, large glaciers still pushed out into the valley from deep clefts in both mountain ranges. Moraines from these flows are responsible for damming the waters that are now Lindbergh and Holland lakes plus several other, smaller ponds.

Today the trout often undertake spawning migrations of 125 miles or more in the Flathead drainage. They are impeded in their movements up the Swan from Flathead Lake by a dam at Bigfork, but they do make significant runs out of Swan Lake, located several miles above the dam. The majority of the migratory cutthroat have been all but replaced by rainbows. The adfluvial strain has been mostly eliminated by the dominance of brook trout. The spawning activity that still occurs usually takes place in the spring through early summer but varies a good deal depending on altitude, longitude, and water characteristics. When water temperatures are near fifty degrees Fahrenheit, spawning begins to take place. Cutthroat have been known to spawn in midsummer in some high mountain lakes. During the summer the trout will establish feeding stations. Sexually mature cutthroat may be as small as six inches in river-dwelling strains and average over a foot in lacustrine-adfluvial populations. There are more than three females to every male. A one-pound female lays between one thousand and fifteen hundred eggs. Spawning is tough work, and less than one-fifth of the fish repeat the process in following seasons.

Of interest to the fly fisher is the fact that large cutthroat prefer pools and align vertically in the water column. This requires more energy than hiding near the bottom with the bull trout but serves a couple of purposes. The ease in obtaining food on the surface more than compensates for the additional energy expenditure, and chances of becoming a bull trout meal are lowered considerably. Cutthroat are primarily invertebrate feeders, which goes a long way to explain their eagerness to hit a dry fly. They may have evolved this behavior in order to avoid competition with bull trout and northern squawfish, both highly piscivorous species.

As a general rule, westslope cutthroat prefer mayflies and dipterans, or true flies, followed by caddis, especially the larger fish.

The bigger the trout, the more diverse the diet. This includes terrestrials such as grasshoppers, ants, and beetles. Insect hatches on the Swan are similar to those on the Middle Fork of the Flathead, with slightly better numbers of mayflies, more hoppers, and a few less stoneflies buzzing about. Like other rivers in northwest Montana, with the exception of the Kootenai, the fish are not exceptionally sophisticated. They have not seen a lot of imitations ranging in size from 2/0 to 26. The trout are not as plentiful nor as large as their southwestern counterparts. The real key to success is approximating size, shape, and color, in that order. Persistence and reasonably accurate casting tend to help the process along.

The upper Flathead River basin, including the Swan, is the largest stronghold for the trout. Cutthroat are still found in eighty-five percent of their historic range here, with the South Fork of the Flathead offering the most secure habitat, in part because of the construction of Hungry Horse Dam and because the Bob Marshall Wilderness complex protects most of the river's headwaters. Nineteen of the twenty-two genetically pure lake-dwelling westslope populations are in Glacier National Park.

Aside from logging, one of the major threats to westslope cutthroat is hybridization with golden, rainbow, and Yellowstone cutthroat trout, all of which are present in at least a limited extent in the Swan drainage. One lake in the Mission Mountains contains a race of cutthroat that have a decidedly yellow cast to their flanks. Years ago goldens were planted here. Gee, I wonder what happened. Aside from these threats, mining (especially placer operations), oil and gas exploration, water diversions, and livestock overgrazing can also do a number on cutthroat populations.

There is an ice-cold Mission Mountain Wilderness tributary with a fair number of eight- to twelve-inch cutthroat. Wet wading is an extreme experience, but a Royal Wulff launched into bubbling plunge pools, along runs, and over riffles will take trout with delightful consistency. The little silvery fish fight like mad in the current. They are sleek but muscular, with bright orange slashes beneath their jaws. Nice trout swimming away, with silent, mysterious forest (where it hasn't been ravaged by logging) slashing far into the sky in the heart of prime grizzly habitat. Fishing here is a primitive, slightly spooky experience, and bear vibes are on the prowl. Casting while looking over your shoulder because the hair on the nape of your neck is standing just a touch is fantastic fun. Playing around with innate fears. Highly recommended.

One survey conducted on Swan tributaries in the 1980s revealed that brook trout accounted for ninety-one percent of the catch. Average size was 8.1 inches for brookies, 7.4 for cutthroat, 5.2 for rainbows, and 6.8 for bull trout.

Where logging has run amok and the resulting loss of canopy has led to stream warming, sedimentation, channel braiding, and other awful stuff, brook trout usually take over, especially in the lower-elevation and gradient reaches of tributaries. Studies indicate that cutthroat are caught twice as easily as the brook trout, so clear-cutting more or less spells death to the westslope subspecies.

One promising note is that cutthroat respond rapidly to habitat restoration and special regulations, including reduced possession limits and catch-and-release fishing. Scott Rumsey, a biologist for the MDFWP, has been working on the drafting and implementation of a fisheries management plan for the Swan drainage with emphasis on producing a high-quality wild-trout fishery that places a high priority on both cutthroat and bull trout.

Initial plans call for a rebuilding of the native westslope cutthroat numbers in the river and tributaries to provide a fishery in the Swan with a catch rate of one cutthroat per four hours and a population level exceeding 250 per mile. Adfluvial cutthroat would be reestablished by removing brook trout from selected tributaries, it is to be hoped with imprinting occurring in the new cutthroat. This means they would be able to detect characteristics of their natal streams and return to spawn generation after generation. Attempts will be made to try to modify timber cutting to lessen riparian corridor impacts, to improve fish passage at the Bigfork Dam (this may not be feasible at the present with the predatious lake trout out of control in Flathead Lake and the Flathead River system), and to monitor catch-and-release practices.

The temptation both for those who know a river well and for those who have never fished a stream is to find someone with a raft and float the water. The Swan can be floated, but because of the sometimes braided channel and the many downed trees and logjams, a casual outing of a few miles can quickly turn into an afternoon of misery. The few area residents that occasionally glide down the river have been known to pack small chain saws or hand saws. Fish and Game biologists float pretty much the same sections of river each year while conducting population surveys or checking habitat, and even they are sometimes forced to portage around obstructions or to cut their way through. Access to the water is available from state campgrounds, from the Swan Highway (209), and from the many bridges that cross the river.

The river is not difficult to wade, with its stretches of wide gravel, rock-and-sand beaches, or grassy banks. There are also some tough stretches of dense timber and brush, but some careful wading can skirt these nasty affairs. Grizzlies and black bears are present at times, as are all sorts of smaller mammals. A day's worth of wading will include thousands of deer and elk tracks, an eagle or two gliding far overhead, and the jackhammer sound of a red-shafted flicker or perhaps a pileated woodpecker banging its head against a dead tree in search of bugs. I've spotted kingfishers perched on branches over the water intently scanning the current for a likely fishy victim. Once in a while along a quiet backwater, I spot a tall, stately, slim heron standing dead-still, almost invisible along the bank. Deer flies and mosquitoes are also present in flesh-chewing numbers. Walking into the river to escape them can be uncomfortable, but with a bit of bug spray the pests cease to be much of a problem when casting.

Make enough noise and the bears usually execute a mad crashing scramble to avoid contact. The one animal I worry about is a big cat. The mountain lion has become a serious nuisance in northwest Montana. Every year a few children, pets, and marauding tourists are attacked by the stealthy cats. One lion stalked a child as he walked a trail near a road in Glacier, pounced, and caused some severe lacerations and punctures. While fishing along the Rocky Mountain Front one spring, I climbed out of my float tube to take a bankside break. My companion pointed to some horses on a hill that were formed in a circle with the colts in the center. I could hear their hooves stomping on the hard ground. I was advised to "get the hell back into the water." My friend had spotted a cat that swiftly disappeared into the tall brush that grew in my direction. Being a predator is one thing, being the prey is another. I moved with impressive alacrity, the hair on my neck and arms standing straight up, even in the harsh wind. The track of the cat is often sighted in mud wallows along the Swan River. I keep my eyes and ears open.

When fishing the river, but not for bull trout, which will be dealt with shortly if only for archival purposes, I carry a 5-weight with a double-taper line. A nine-foot leader tapered to 4X or 5X is adequate. During the summer the stream is a pleasure to wade wet. For flies I carry my Elk Hair Caddis selection, running from #12–18 and from tan to nearly black. I also carry a good hopper pattern in #6–10, an attractor like a Royal Wulff, a few foam beetles and ants, Adamses in #10–18, Gold-Ribbed Hare's Ears in #12–16, Prince nymphs in #10–14, green Antron emergers in #12–14, a few Sofa Pillows in #6–8, and a couple of Woolly Buggers (weighted, of course) in #6–8. A #4 brown stonefly nymph on a 4XL hook will take fish, but this is hard and often tedious fishing. If I cannot catch fish with these I give up.

If no fish are spotted working the surface, I start out with the Hare's Ears or the Antron emerger. Then I shift to the Elk Hairs and hoppers in the heat of summer. If this fails, I switch to the trusty Bugger, which will normally, at the very least, locate some good trout, usually rainbows or cutthroat but occasionally a bull trout if the drift is along the bottom. Everything is straightforward on the river. A modicum of stealth, an accurate cast to promising water, and a pinch of line control is about all that's needed — except for the bull trout.

Fishing for these fish with dry flies is like sending a Mother's Day card when a bomb is required, and the drastic methods work well for big rainbows also. There have been rare instances when

I've caught smaller bulls on drys, but the majority of these fish are taken by drifting large streamers down along the bottoms of rocky, uneven, fast runs, through the tails of pools resembling small lakes, and slipped beneath large piles of jammed up logs, trees, and shattered Kevlar kayaks.

Where you find logging, road-building, subdivisions, and other manmade indecencies, you are not likely to locate the big char. In the Swan they hang out in Swan Lake before making a springtime march upstream to isolated sections of clear cold-water tributaries that have appropriate sizes of substrate gravels for redd construction. I've seen redds as large as the roof of a Chevy Suburban and a foot or so deep. Before these moves, you can find the fish paired up and holding quietly in pools near the outlet into the main river. I never fished for the bulls when they were in the tributaries. Some things are best left alone. Three or more bulls usually join forces to make these depressions, often at night with rapid, powerful beatings of their tails as they work lying on their sides.

These are big trout, directly related to brook and lake trout and Arctic char. Over the years the fish I've taken average over twenty-six inches and seven pounds, with the biggest over thirty inches and ten pounds. They have been documented in past years in the twenty-pound range, but these are rare. Anything over ten is a good fish.

There is a spot on the Swan well above the lake and far from the highway, through clear-cuts, devil's club, swamp, and thick brush (a bitch of a hike, but part of the experience I guess), that I fish each season, usually around late July or early August. The stretch always produced bulls. I allowed myself two per year: enough to satisfy my wonder and curiosity and still leave them pretty much alone on their spawning peregrinations. The place I worked was a prime location, so I counted on taking my brace of bulls (which were carefully revived and promptly released) in a day's determined casting (read twelve hours and over seven hundred drifts).

The fish stack up along a couple of hundred yards of eroding gravel bank that is covered with thick grass up on top. The spawning tributary is just upstream. The river rushes over a wide gravel shelf before plunging into a short, wide, emerald pool and then squeezes into a fifteen-foot-wide run of four feet or so deep and maybe one hundred yards long. Perfect stuff for the bulls. Wading across the river and creeping up along the bank, I could see the fish holding along the bottom in the relative calm. Fish from eighteen inches to more than two feet were visible. Lots of them.

The cast is fifty, sixty feet quartering upstream with a ten-foot 7-weight sinking tip and a nine-foot 8-weight rod. This makes for easier line pickup. I like a leader of seven or eight feet tapering to a delicate 0X. The fish have large razor-sharp teeth, the streambed is abrasive, and the trout are strong. This holds true for large cutts and rainbow, which also have sharp teeth. Depending on the location of the cast, a number of mends are required to give the streamer—a 1/0 red-and-white woolhead bendback is my pattern of preference—an opportunity to work down deep. If the drift is right and justly proper, I can feel the streamer bouncing against the rocks as it swings past me on downstream. Always let the pattern swing in the current for a few seconds before making swift strips and then the next cast.

I've never taken a bull on the first dozen or even five dozen casts. There seems to be some time needed for me to get in sync with the process, the rhythm and concentration that connect me through the moving water to the fish. When a bull hits, the strike is savage, ripping the rod down into the water and almost out of my hands. The fish often roll up to the surface when they take, the bright pink of their bellies flashing briefly before the trout runs downstream at a steady, determined pace. Even a bull of four or five pounds will pull into the backing. Anything larger and I am forced to follow the fish downstream. A couple of good runs and the bulls usually come into shallow water, but they are not finished. They cannot be horsed in. Within seconds they spot me and race off, angled to make the most of the current, heads shaking and water spraying. The sight of such a large fish suddenly galvanized into a riotous, thrashing dash for freedom often catches me by surprise.

If this run is weathered, the trout normally come grudgingly to hand in a time of tense maneuvering that is a nervous compromise between the strength of the stressed tippet and my ability to reach out and grab the bull trout's tail. If I'm successful, the fish holds steady; the energy returning to its solid frame is palpable.

They do not color up as brightly as brook trout do, but the whites and blacks of their fins are as distinct. Their backs are dark green reflecting golds and sunshine silvers. Large orange spots and a blaze-pink belly complete the scheme. The head is long and flattened, an evolutionary adaptation to facilitate its predilection for eating other fish. The head shape and greater mean size are among the chief morphological differences between bulls and their close and often-confused-with relation, the Dolly Varden. What you catch in northwest Montana are bull trout. What you catch somewhere else might be Dollies.

A bull trout's coloration allows it to blend in perfectly with its surroundings. One September day on a tributary of the North Fork of the Flathead River I accompanied MDFWP biologist Tom Weaver as he electrofished a section of stream to determine the number of juvenile bull trout present. Near the end of the stretch the current shocked a huge bull that swirled violently right between us. The fish nearly knocked Weaver over and sprayed water everywhere. The trout weighed in at over twelve pounds, and we were standing right next to the creature, which held dead still. It was invisible to our eyes, focused intently on the streambed.

Any large streamer would take the fish, provided the fake is bounced right to their noses. They will follow a fly after it has passed over them but, based on my experience, bull trout do not chase offerings that are very far to the right or left of them. Red-and-white was by far the best combination, probably because this resembles a small cutthroat or rainbow as it swims in the flickering currents.

Deep runs are the "easiest" to work. Beneath logjams is always a logical place to probe, but try and drag a big fish out of the submerged tangle of debris. Weaver tells of diving in the river by one logjam where a big bull trout shot out from the dark to examine him. The sight of a huge fish with a wide-open tooth-lined mouth was unsettling, according to the biologist.

Timing was everything in bull trout fishing. Begin too soon and you were captive of a river gone mad with runoff. Make your humble presentations too late in the summer and the bulls had secretly vanished up their special little tributaries to breed in secret. When the water dropped, sometime in late June or early July up until late August, you had a chance at finding the fish. I'll continue my yearly trips to fish for the secretive bulls, but I'll worry more about their declining numbers in the Flathead drainage, and I also worry about morons in pickup trucks herding the large but fragile salmonids into nets stretched across their spawning streams. The macho, courageous jerks do this under the cover of darkness, as I'm sure they do most of their subnormal activities. You run into this human detritus in bars around the valley drunkenly bragging about their heroic exploits. One pair showed off several of the dead bulls they'd dragged into a bar in a gunnysack. Later I heard that their truck was discovered with four flat tires. How does this nonsense happen, man? I really wonder.

Aside from the destruction wreaked by poachers, the other main threats in the Swan and the Flathead are logging and development.

Intensive clear-cutting and the attendant road-building have caused a great deal of damage to the Swan fishery as well as to the visual quality of the valley. Extensive clear-cuts are visible up and down the river climbing the steep slopes of both the Mission and Swan mountains. Some logging even occurred illegally in the Mission Mountain Wilderness some years ago.

When clear-cutting and road-building take place on steep, highly erosible slopes, heavy rains and spring runoff deliver tons of sediment to stream channels. This in turn suffocates bull and west-slope cutthroat trout eggs and emerging fry. The most recent example of this type of calamity occurred this spring in Overwhich Creek, a tributary of the West Fork of the Bitterroot River. A clear-cut slope slumped, sending tons of sediment and gravel into Overwhich, wiping out a population of cutthroat. The stuff also clogged the bottom of a downstream reservoir and destroyed large numbers

*Logging and related road damage in the Swan River drainage.*

of invertebrates in the West Fork. Juvenile trout were forced out of the West Fork into the main river, where they were easy prey for larger trout. In part because of intense public outcry, the forest service has promised to use large amounts of its resources and manpower to speed up the recovery process, which may take several years or more.

A similar incident occurred on Plum Creek Timber Company land along the West Fork of Jim Creek. Large amounts of sediment and other debris washed off a steeply clear-cut slope and destroyed one year's class of bull trout. Spring runoff has since flushed the stream-course, but similar events in the drainage could have further disastrous consequences for the bull trout. The cumulative impacts of such blowouts are not yet fully understood by biologists.

An article I wrote on the mess for a 1991 issue of *Fly Fisherman* was not received with high praise by Plum Creek officials. In response, they flew the magazine's editor, John Randolph, and me out to Jim Creek. Their sincerity and arguments were persuasive. I began believing that they were committed to a new "environmentally sensitive" form of logging.

"We now manage for sociopolitical as well as economic concerns," said Plum Creek Director of Operations Bill Parson. "We did not think that way in the past. We have tried to use Jim Creek as a learning tool. Hey! We were beating our heads against a wall doing things the old way. The public is not buying it anymore."

The tour demonstrated a variety of lands managed for a succession of growth, new ways of preventing sediment from washing off hillsides and roads and into streams, wildlife management programs, and different approaches to logging. Talking with Parson and other Plum Creek workers left me with the impression that we all wish to enjoy the same things in the outdoors, that we really were not so far apart in our viewpoints. John Randolph thought so, too.

But I start to wonder when I read about the company handing out fliers with paychecks at their Columbia Falls plant that say "The liberal politicians are trying to take away our reasons for living in Montana. Let's not let it happen," and concerning a scheduled protimber rally, "There should be NO excuse for not being there. Your jobs, recreation and the very reason why you live here depend on it."

The flier went on to lambaste Democrat congressional representative Pat Williams, who was running against his Republican counterpart, Ron Marlenee. Williams favors more wilderness, while Marlenee favors anything related to big business (that is, unless clear-cutting would degrade the view from outside a window of his residence at a Montana ski resort. Marlenee had this logging stopped immediately, which flies in the face of his vociferous support of expanded clear-cutting in the West. I guess when it's in your own backyard, things are different).

The flier added "Pat free in '93" as part of a lengthy list of slogans: "You'll need a job, Pat. I heard the Sierra Club is hiring."

Plum Creek officials termed the incident "unfortunate." Williams's spokesman cited state election law prohibiting companies from including with paychecks "the name of any candidate or any political mottoes, devices or arguments containing threats or promises (express or implied) calculated or intended to influence the political opinions or actions of the employees." Williams won anyway.

This, coupled with the sick feeling I get in my stomach every time I look up at one of Plum Creek's new clear-cuts, makes me wonder if the people I spent time with at Jim Creek really do love the land as much as they say.

The other big landowner in the Swan is the U.S. Forest Service, and they have been brought under some semblance of control by the determined efforts of local grassroots environmental groups and concerned individuals. Only 17.1 million board feet of timber were sold, compared to a target of 75 million, during fiscal year 1992 in the Flathead National Forest, part of which borders a sizable portion of the Swan River. Logging used to be in the 100-million-board-foot range annually but is now about one-third that level. And even area loggers are on the forest service's case, as exemplified by one regional logger in a letter that said in part:

". . . Instead of the Forest Service trying to work with small opera-tors to keep them in business and off welfare, the Forest Service has made a concerted effort to shut us all down. Until there is a change in the attitude of the Forest Service from pro-big-business to fairness on all levels, maybe the forest would be better off taking a rest so the trees can grow a little."

Testify, brother!

Clear-cutting may be as big a threat as ever, but at least there is the illusion of control out there in the old-growth forest. Not so with the destruction being visited on western Montana by the greedy hordes of realtors, developers, and moneylenders that have descended on this part of the world like a malignant clutch of maggots. From early morning until late at night there are com-mercials on television showing people standing on tops of soon-to-be-sold homes, reworking tired-out World War II victory slogans into pathetic sales pitches, or presenting slickly dressed hucksters promoting the development potential of a prime (and formerly unspoiled) stretch of river land.

These people are completely out of control. Real estate prices have doubled in a couple of years. These venal clowns are award-ing themselves "Good-Guy Realtor of the Month" honors on an hourly basis. There are so many people getting into the frenzied insanity that commissions are being split into shares too small to buy a boring lunch at a local Tofu-and-Bean-Sprouts-R-Us restau-rant. There are so many golf courses out here the elk and deer and bears are often seen feeding on the fairways. Where the hell else can they eat? Their habitat is being bulldozed for another championship 18. Fore! Zoning changes are the only solution, but the real estate guys are on all of the committees designed to study and change this situation. Kind of your basic fox-guarding-the-henhouse scenario.

Climb any mountain surrounding the Flathead (or the Swan or Bitterroot or Missoula) Valley and look down at night on the bright glow of lights and the unending hum of cars and trucks. In what was once an unspoiled stretch of the Swan Valley a major motel chain has erected a modern facility replete with gaudy yellow sign and blacktopped parking lot. May it die a swift and painful financial death. As writer Bob Jones said one day, "Good country . . . it's all going or gone, John. Enjoy what is left with your kids while you still can."

Bob is right, but this is where Lynda and I are raising our family. We aren't leaving and we aren't going down without a fight. Maybe we can't stop the avaricious horde, but we sure can give them a hard time.

But I digress from the fishing once again.

The river above Condon turns into a much smaller forested stream. While the pools here are not large, there is sufficient pocket water to hold some fair-sized brook and cutthroat trout. One section below Lindbergh Lake is ideal 1-weight water. Wading up to my chest through narrow channels and casting a Royal Humpy dead upstream tight to the mossy banks is wildly productive. Fighting the native trout on a light rod at almost eye level in the heart of an ancient forest is entertaining. The entire perspective on fishing changes. Brookies and cutts do not jump much, but when they splash water in my face as they resist the tension of the line just a few feet away, there is a certain immediacy, a subtle but discernible shift in my outlook. I almost feel like a trout myself, or like an omniscient third party watching my angling self casting to, hooking, playing, and then releasing little eight- and nine-inch trout. All my other self can see is the fish fighting, the rod and line, and my head, shoulders, and arms. A most curious and oddly disorienting vision. High weirdness submerged in a trout stream.

When I first worked this stretch below Lindbergh Lake in the early seventies, I was unaware that the lake was named for the aviator Charles A. Lindbergh, who visited the area in 1927 with his aide, Lieutenant Donald E. Keyhoe, as they barnstormed the country in the *Spirit of St. Louis.* Landing in Butte, Lindbergh planned to escape his hectic schedule and visit Glacier Park. Flying toward Glacier, Lindbergh and his companion cruised past the Swans and the Missions. They spent several hours zipping between the peaks of Glacier and down its glacial valleys and just above the surface of some of its turquoise lakes. One lake high in the Missions had attracted his attention. Known as Elbow back then, it was changed to Lindbergh when area residents learned of the flier's infatuation. Lindbergh visited the lake in the autumn of that year, hosted by several prominent state residents.

What this has to do with fly fishing I'm not sure, but I would have liked to have seen the Swan Valley back then before all the clear-cutting and development.

The Swan River presents a number of personalities to the fly fisher, from the timbered, small mountain stream to a wider almost freestone affair farther down, to the wide, slow, glassy river below Swan Lake, and then finally to the brief fling with whitewater craziness below the Bigfork Dam. But my favorite side of the river is the one that twists and glides over the gravel and stone riverbed, the part of the river that is surrounded by grassy banks that give way slowly to thick pine forest and then to ice-carved mountains that rip almost straight up from the valley floor.

The riffles always seem to hold plenty of cutthroat and rainbows that make up for their small size with a carefree willingness to pounce on a dry fly. The deep, swinging undercut banks and the pools behind the logjams hold larger, harder-to-catch fish.

A bad drift pushed into artificial behavior by the drag of the countless fingers of current braiding the water column spooks the trout. To catch these fish when they are feeding on top, the caster must consider all facets of the river—the flow, the breeze, where the line will pass, the spot where the trout is holding.

Because the river often turns so swiftly from one side of the stream-course to the other, a long cast might be only forty feet or less. Sometimes I have to kneel in the water with the curve of dry rock between me and the run where some nice trout are feeding. Wading closer puts down the wild fish for a long time. The line shoots out over the beach and lands upstream in the heart of the main current seam. The Elk Hair Caddis closes on the first and largest of the trout. The sun is low over my shoulder in the west, and I can see into the water. The cutthroat comes up, takes, and I hand-set the hook, flipping a small stone that the line had worked under during the drift. The fish shakes and splashes and runs right past me in the river, glowing dark silver as it drags a bow of slack behind. I hastily crank line in and play the cutthroat on the reel. It comes easily to my knees in the shallow water.

Certainly over a foot, maybe fifteen inches, but this one is not marked against the rod. Instead, the trout is quickly separated from the hook and released, and another cast flies out toward the head of the pool. The light is fading fast and there are still more trout feeding above me.

# BLACKFOOT RIVER

*L*ynda and I were working on a casual buzz, sedately fueled by some beers and vodka tonics earlier this afternoon, while the steaks burned over the fire. The North Fork of the Blackfoot rolled on its sweet way right behind us. We could hear the steady swirlings and surges of the water as it rushed over the colorful boulder-and-gravel streambed and cut into the root-choked banks.

The sun had disappeared somewhere over the Mission Mountains, unseen off in the west. Caddis were coming off the river and flitting around in the bushes and in the warm night air above us. I built a couple more drinks—plenty of vodka, a splash of tonic, and a big slice of lime over cubed ice—and we talked and laughed about some outrageous brown trout fishing we'd had on a little stream over a touch east of here somewhere earlier in the day, and we laughed a little about a great little bar in Helmville, and we laughed some more just because we were alone together and someone else was taking care of our three wonderful, delightful, well-behaved children.

Ostensibly we were over in this country fishing and taking pictures of the Blackfoot for this book, but things did not work out quite that way and we spent most of our time catching cutthroat and rainbows in the river that was chattering away behind us. And that was more than all right because the Blackfoot wasn't going anywhere and we'd be back again soon. Just ask the boys in Trixi's Bar over by Ovando. They were hip to our con and laughed a little bit, too.

*The Blackfoot River.*

The Blackfoot has always been one of my favorite rivers. In the early seventies I would drive up Highway 200 from Missoula on a warm afternoon and work caddis and hopper patterns along the crystal jade (cream jade near the end of spring runoff) edges of deep pools and current seams that were only a few yards from the road. The trout always cooperated, usually surging up from the gravel-and-sand bottom to smash the fly in a shower of spray before jumping and running for a little while.

The only people I saw fishing this stretch were floaters in cheap yellow rafts like the one I owned, a sorry affair that leaked slowly but steadily at a rate that often meant one of our number would be forced to abandon ship near the end of the float so that we would not founder before take-out. This was all right because the chosen victim was always set loose with a cooler of cold beer to wait for our eventual return. We, the sodden crew, even tried to drop the chosen one off at a promising run or pool, considerate companions that we were.

At the height of one such float on a glorious, hot July day, we were taking trout with some consistency on hoppers when we happened to float past some naked hipsters bathing on a far bank. We had long hair too, but obviously did not radiate the proper peace-and-love, mother earth vibes (we did have a battery-powered cassette deck playing John Mayall's "Turning Point"—cutting-edge raft technology). The husband-father-tribal-leader noticed our fly rods and made a penetrating observation along the lines of "Nice day for the fish, too. All God's creatures deserve to live." We were practicing catch-and-release and exchanged raised eyebrows among ourselves.

This type of situation, involving the frequently brain-dead self-righteous, always leaves me gasping for an appropriate response. Not so my friend in the bow of the raft. With the quickest of pickups and briefest of backcasts he launched his hopper like a shot into the boulder, inches from where Moon Father was holding forth. The hook pinged off the rock. The look of surprise and wonder at this act of aggression was priceless: open mouth, slack jaw, wide eyes.

You had to be there, as they say, but this superb cast made our day in a simpleminded, easily pleased sort of way.

The Blackfoot has its beginnings near Rogers Pass on the Continental Divide, not far from the Scapegoat Wilderness to the north. The Missouri and Dearborn rivers are on the other side of the mountains. The river runs for a hundred miles down the mountains through timbered, agricultural, and then timbered land before squeezing through a bouldery canyonlike stretch on the final pitch to the Clark Fork at the mill town of Bonner.

The Blackfoot is not all that difficult to wade from the headwaters down to its confluence with the North Fork at River Junction, provided some observation and caution are employed. Felt soles and a wading staff help, too. Below here and especially from the Roundup Bar down to Bonner, wading is best left to world-class whackos like most of my friends, and even myself on daring occasions. Death by slipping, sliding, tumbling, and finally drowning is possible in this stretch. The mean September flow at the Clark Fork is 1,000 cfs.

From a few miles south of Clearwater Junction up to Rogers Pass, Highway 200 travels over an uneven landscape of glacial moraines. Ice- and rock-gouged low spots are indicated by small ponds and marshes. Mounded areas contain rocks and boulders. The pine-forested hills south of the junction are part of an ancient moraine that probably dates back to the Bull Lake glaciation period, 70,000 to 100,000 years ago. Below this location the highway follows the valley of an old meltwater stream onto an open outwash plain. Near Clearwater Junction, large boulders dropped from icebergs floating in glacial Lake Missoula are visible. This lake covered much of the region fifteen thousand years ago, frequently blowing out a natural ice dam as many as forty-one times and sending up to five hundred cubic miles of water in a wall two thousand feet high that rushed west in the general direction of present-day Spokane. Numerous shoreline ridges left from the lake are still visible on the hills surrounding Missoula.

Between Missoula and Ovando the highway traverses the Garnet Range and its sharply tilted sedimentary rock layers. This is the north edge of the Sapphire tectonic block that moved into Montana off the top of the Idaho batholith possibly on a bed of molten granite magma 75 million years ago. The folded layers are the block's leading edge. Most of the mountains in the Blackfoot drainage are Precambrian sedimentary rock that began as mud and sand over a billion years ago.

A large fault running in a northwest direction in the Potomoc area about twenty miles northeast of Bonner is responsible for periodic earthquakes in the region that rattle homes and other structures as far away as Missoula on occasion. This causes a friend of mine a good bit of anxiety. Murderers, the threat of nuclear war, and the possibility of hideous plagues are minor concerns compared to the terror engendered by demon earthquakes in the mind of this friend, who is largely given credit for causing seismologists at Cal State to resort to prerecorded messages concerning such earthly activity. Backbreaking phone bills are of little importance to my buddy when it comes to gathering up-to-date information on earthquakes. He drove the boys at Cal State nuts.

He claims to be much better now, but a recent visit found him highly agitated over a headline about seismic activity in the Palm Springs area.

The Blackfoot Valley above Clearwater Junction was the scene for huge rivers of ice pouring out of rugged canyons, which gave way to piedmont glaciers or stagnant ice, some as much as several miles wide. Meltwater choked with sediment and larger debris scattered sand and gravels across the valley, creating outwash plains. Ovando sits atop such a feature between the two morainal hummocks. The highway cuts through glacial till.

The resurgence in mining activity above Lincoln results from masses of molten granite magma as much as several miles thick intruding into sedimentary slabs of rock making up part of the overthrust belt. The magma brought small amounts of valuable metallic minerals with it.

Obviously, the life of the Blackfoot River is intrinsically connected to this geology, which is largely responsible for the wide diversity of water types and habitat for salmonid species including browns, rainbows, hybrids, brookies, cutthroats, and bull trout, plus mountain whitefish. The last three are native to the river. There are also suckers and smaller forage fish that provide excellent table fare for the larger trout.

An extremely generalized breakdown of the fish populations along the river's course would include westslope cutthroat in the headwaters above Lincoln and in most tributaries, brown trout from here down to around Cottonwood Creek, and rainbows on to the confluence with the Clark Fork, including the Clearwater River. Bull trout, an extremely threatened species in the river, are occasionally found in the river and in tributaries like the North Fork.

One survey turned up an average of less than fifty rainbows larger than twelve inches per thousand feet of lower river. There were more than two hundred rainbows between five and twelve inches on average, though. Ten cutthroat greater than six inches was about average in this part of the stream. A very few brown trout were found. In a stretch near the Scotty Brown Bridge not far from Ovando, the numbers were 2.3 rainbows greater than four-teen inches and 34 between four and fourteen inches, 23 browns greater than six inches, and 2.3 bull trout in the same range.

Some of the larger hatches include salmonflies from late May into July moving upriver as far as the North Fork before the golden stones begin to predominate slightly later in the season. Peak time for salmonflies is often peak time for runoff, making the fishing tough. One year in four is considered a good average for timing the hatch with clearing and dropping water conditions.

During periods of high flow and turbidity, a large nymph crawled along the bottom toward shore will often take big fish on a surprisingly steady basis. They can see and sense the big bugs and frequently hold in areas of calm behind rocks and other ob-structions waiting for the lumbering creatures. Don't abandon hope just because the water looks badly out of shape. Spend an hour or two with this plodding form of fishing. The results are often worth the drudgery of sinking-tip madness.

The skwala, a gray medium-sized stonefly, appears in March and April, providing good action during a window of opportunity that usually opens for an hour or so around midafternoon. As the nymphs begin to crawl toward shoreline rocks, the trout key on the vulnerable bugs. Dry imitations work particularly well, and some of the largest trout of the season are found looking up during this hatch.

Ameletus appear after the skwalas and again in the fall. These mayflies are larger on average than the blue-winged olives, and a #12–14 dark gray dun would appear to be the proper match. On the Blackfoot, with almost any dry it is always better to think big, especially in current seams and riffles. Use a #10 or even #8 for a #12. On this river a larger tie is more effective at bringing the trout up through the water column to take on the surface.

As with most western rivers, *Baetis* make a spring and fall ap-pearance. BWOs in #16–18 and shaded to the dark gray side of olive are reasonable choices. Nine-foot leaders down to 5X or 6X handle most situations.

A box of Elk Hair Caddis from #10–16 in tan through black covers most of the Trichoptera action throughout the season. Fall caddis in #8–10 (Blackfoot measurement) are dependable from mid-September into October. I like to tie these with a bright orange chenille body, medium cree hackle, and tan wing. The combination has consistently taken trout on rivers throughout the state.

Tricos also intrigue the trout starting after runoff and working well into fall. A #22–24 spinner or even a black midge will goad the fish into taking. A black-bodied spinner with white Z-lon wings seems to be the most productive pattern, though a long leader with a fine tippet coupled with a well-placed delicate cast are equally important to an individual's success during this hatch.

Large bushy versions of attractors like Royal and Gray Wulffs (gray is superb on overcast days), Humpies, and Trudes worked in the riffles and through deep runs will normally produce trout even during the height of a bright summer day. The broken current provides adequate cover and a sense of security for rainbows (and the rare brown). Plenty of floatant, Gehrke's Gink comes to mind, worked into the fly is a requirement for a lengthy and successful float. The fly must be on the water for a long time to allow the fish a chance to rise up from the depths and take. This is an agonizing process to watch as the silver form gradually takes on definition, mouth agape. The first few fish are often missed due to eagerness on the fly fisher's part.

Terrestrials like grasshoppers, dark beetles, and brown-black ants are good as soon as the water drops and the weather warms to summertime levels. Hoppers should be fished with a bang, plopped and crashed into grassy banks and onto the water's surface. The rattier and more chewed up the fly, the better it seems to work.

Weighted nymphs like Hare's Ears and Princes also turn trout, especially in the riffles and runs. Unfortunately, the noble whitefish has a predilection for these imitations. Because this species greatly outnumbers trout in most Montana rivers, nymphing can turn into a whitefish extravaganza. These natives fight well but have never truly captured my angling imagination.

As always with the browns, and to a lesser extent the rainbows, large streamers fished slightly upstream, tight to the bank, then down through runs and across the depths of pools produce some of the best fish. Woolly Buggers in #2–6, heavily weighted at the head, and worked in a swimming up-and-down motion never fail. A few strands of Flashabou don't hurt, either. Yellow Marabou Muddlers and, in extreme cases of large-trout fever, olive brown sculpins, also entice the browns. Occasionally a bull trout will hammer one of these. The species can exceed ten pounds and will fight below-surface downstream, taking full advantage of the current. Because of its threatened status, quickly play a bull and then carefully revive and release it.

Veteran guide Paul Roos, who knows this river as well as anyone, lists a number of problems facing the Blackfoot, including timber-cutting and residential development.

"Montana as a whole and the Blackfoot in particular are threatened by subdivisions," said Roos. "And logging and the road-building that goes with it worries me, but I guess I'd have to say that mining and proposed mining like the one above Lincoln may pose the greatest threat to the river. The future is definitely uncertain concerning the Blackfoot."

The history of Montana is linked to the mining industry. Millions of tons of precious metals have been dug, blasted, and filtered from the ground and nearby streams. Enough gold has been mined to sink a fleet of cargo ships. The same holds true, only more so, for lesser lights like silver and copper. And rarer metals of equal or greater value than gold are now coming into their own in the eyes of mining company executives and investors on world markets.

Propelled by the 1872 Mining Law, an act many feel is nothing more than a federal giveaway program, speculation in precious metals is undergoing renewed interest. Everywhere you look these days, some mining operation has its eyes on a mother lode of staggering value. Millions of dollars of silver ore may be extracted from beneath the Cabinet Mountains Wilderness by the Noranda Mineral Corporation. Exploratory blasting has already violated state hard-rock-mining pollution laws and polluted nearby streams. Gold fever is rising once again in the headwaters of the Blackfoot River at a project proposed by Phelps-Dodge that would level a mountain in the headwaters. More gold-digging is proposed in a joint venture by the Canadian firm Manhattan Minerals and Ernest K. Lehmann and Associates of Minneapolis. And Crown Butte Mines Inc. of Butte wants to dig for gold in the Beartooth Mountains only miles from Yellowstone Park, and the Absaroka-Beartooth Wilderness is just two miles away. Mining scars will be visible from both locations. Pollution could harm the Yellowstone River fishery.

Bring on the Mongol hordes. Slaughter all the salmonids. Sack the trout streams. The hell with the aesthetics.

So what does all of this have to do with trout and fly fishing along the Blackfoot and other parts of the mineral-rich West? Almost everything in some river drainages.

American Rivers, the river-preservation organization, listed the Blackfoot as one of the ten most endangered rivers in North America, along with the likes of the Columbia, Snake, Beaverkill, and the Colorado as it cuts through the Grand Canyon, to name a few. American Rivers says the Blackfoot "has been a river in decline for decades," due to degradation from timber-cutting, cattle grazing, farming, recreation overuse in spots, and mining.

Other environmental groups have asked the forest service to step in and protect the beleaguered stream, and to draft a comprehensive, integrated management plan that addresses future needs and problems.

Sloppy disposal of tailings, settling-pond failure, the leaching of cyanide into the aquifer, soil erosion—any one of these can spell disaster for trout populations not just for a year or two but for decades. Look what has happened around Butte. Nearby streams are so full of heavy metals that if any trout did live in some of these waters they would probably sink. The entire region west to Anaconda is the nation's largest Super Fund site.

Does this renewed interest in mining in Montana mean yet another nail in the coffin of the state's world-class trout fishery?

At first glance, the answer is quite possibly yes, but there are strong indications both in and outside the mining industry that positive change and serious commitment to the wild resource may avert disaster.

The best place to start (and the most alarming from the standpoint of a fly fisher) is with the controversial 1872 Mining Law that was passed in part to help fuel the homesteading drive in the West that had its genesis in the 1862 Homestead Act. The 1873 law allows miners to purchase mining claims on federal lands at a price of only $2.50 per acre for placer claims (normally located along stream bottoms) and $5.00 per acre for lode claims. These prices have not changed since the law's inception. Where mining claims occur, mineral development, under the 1872 law, is considered the best and most appropriate use of the land. Some estimates place the amount of land sold thus far under this law at greater than 20 million acres. According to Department of the Interior data, the federal treasury misses out on $880 million per year from lost royalties and lost land value, not to mention the costs of environmental damage. The U.S. Bureau of Mines estimates that twelve thousand miles of streams have contaminated water from past mining activity, not including adjacent habitat destroyed by placer mining.

According to former Secretary of the Interior Stewart Udall, "The most important piece of unfinished business on the nation's resource agenda is the complete replacement of the Mining Law of 1872."

Udall has reason to be concerned. Consider the following abuses listed in an excellent article by Montana Department of Fish, Wildlife and Parks Pollution Control Biologist Glenn Phillips in the March-April 1992 issue of *Fisheries*. Titled "The 1872 Mining Law: Reforming a Dinosaur," Phillips mentions the following:

One western Montana miner is capitalizing on his patented placer claim (purchased at $2.50 per acre) by selling summer homesites along a trout stream. Others are maintaining claim sites as private hunting camps in prime elk country. In Oregon, a portion of the Oregon Dunes Recreation Area was successfully

patented for a total price of $1,950, and the new owners are now
trying to trade or sell the property back to the forest service and
the Bureau of Land Management (BLM) at an asking price of $12
million. A 1989 General Accounting Office report lists values of
lands given away for the going patented price at anywhere from
$200 to $200,000 per acre.

Sounds like a hell of a deal. Where do I sign up?

Outrage over the law is reflected in a poll released in 1992 by
the Northern Plains Resource Council. By a twelve-to-one margin,
state residents wanted to update the patenting provision of the
1872 Mining Law.

Sixty percent of those surveyed agreed that the law needs revi-
sion because it does not require royalty payments to states or the
federal government, and because patent fees have remained un-
changed for more than one hundred years. Over three-fourths of
those polled agreed that hard-rock mining should be at least as
strictly regulated as coal mining.

Seventy-five percent of those surveyed opposed mining that permanently damaged other important natural resource values. The
1872 law gives mining companies the "right to mine" on public
lands regardless of potential environmental damage.

Finally, seventy-eight percent of those surveyed opposed exemptions that let mining companies degrade the water quality in Montana's most pristine streams. Several companies have asked for
exemptions in recent years.

According to EPA findings, the hard-rock-mining industry
creates between one and four *billion* tons of solid waste each year.
Almost no hard-rock mining sites are currently required to be restored to premining conditions. Groundwater impacts are frequently ignored by the BLM. The Mineral Policy Center estimates
the cost of cleaning up historic hard-rock-mining sites at somewhere between $20 and $50 billion.

Sounds gloomy at best. Factor in comments made by the head
of the U.S. Bureau of Mines, T. S. Ary, in a 1992 speech before
a group of miners, loggers, ranchers, farmers, and other advocates
of developing federal land gathered in Denver, and the future looks

grim: "I don't believe in endangered species. I think the only ones are sitting here in this room."

Because the conference was titled the "National Wilderness Conference," Ary mistakenly assumed he was going to be addressing environmentalists. When he found out otherwise he commented, "I thought I was going to come out and be a sacrificial lamb for a bunch of nuts."

"There are a lot of degrading things to the environment—logging, grazing, etcetera—that will heal themselves over time, but mining scars will be with us long after the earth is a cinderball and there is no sun," said Gary LaFontaine, who lives in Deer Lodge, close to the country's largest Super Fund site. "Arco has been charged with the cleanup, but they refuse to pay, saying that they were encouraged by state laws. But they were in charge of the state legislature back then. To say things are a mess is an understatement."

The situation in many cases is as bad as I have detailed, but there are small rays of light shining here and there that give fly fishers and everyone else who cares about the land some cause for optimism.

Legislation (H.R. 2614) has been proposed to amend the 1872 law by Representative Peter DeFazio (a Democrat from Oregon) that would retain the self-initiated claim system but would remove patenting. Other key provisions of the bill include: requiring miners to pay a five percent royalty on gross income from mineral production, resulting in approximately $200 million that could be used in part to restore damaged streams; residential occupancy on mining claims would be prohibited; reclamation and bonding would be required on all mining claims at a level that would restore the land to the same productive uses that existed prior to mining; federal land use agencies would be required to create strict reclamation standards and would be given discretion to weigh proposed mining activities against other resource values and, if necessary, deny mining; miners would be subject to civil and criminal penalties for violations of the revised act, and there would also be provisions for citizen lawsuits.

Sounds great, doesn't it? Unfortunately, there is a very strong core of resistance in both houses of Congress.

Whether the act is ever changed or not, there are other bright moments in the situation. The Pegasus Gold Corporation's Beal Mountain Mine stands as a prime example of what can be accomplished when the mining industry places strong value not only on the minerals beneath the land, but on the land itself.

This mine sits almost on the Continental Divide at about eight thousand feet above sea level in the Pioneer Mountains west of Butte. The region contains the Mount Haggin Game Range and critical winter habitat for elk, deer, moose, and bear. The mine's main source of water comes from German Gulch, which holds a viable population of pure-strain westslope cutthroat trout.

The company tried an approach almost unheard of in the industry. It held numerous meetings with sportsmen and environmental groups, conferred regularly with government agencies, and held a series of public meetings. Acting on all of this input, Pegasus designed what is currently a state-of-the-art mine as far as protecting the environment goes.

Montana native Carson Rife took control of the project with the simple dictum that if any part of mining activity might harm the environment, that work would not be done.

The major problem facing Rife was the possibility of cyanide, used in the leaching process, escaping through the leach pad into the groundwater. The pad was constructed using waterproof compacted clay with a heavy plastic liner on top. In order to avoid an accidental spill into German Gulch, the company made the costly decision to truck the ore uphill, away from the stream. This is the reverse of the more fuel-efficient process of having loaded trucks coast downhill and then expend less fuel going back uphill, empty.

To avoid intense subsurface pressure on the pad from upwelling groundwater, a large drain field was built beneath the pad. And the groundwater runs into a safety pond, which is monitored closely for any signs of cyanide leaks. During construction of the pad, a bulldozer accidentally tore the liner. Instead of patching the tear, the company replaced the entire item at a cost of $400,000.

In order to minimize impacts from the mine on area wildlife, an electrified fence was built prior to the mine's construction around the four-hundred-acre site to keep animals from wandering into the construction zone. A net was placed over the holding pond where the cyanide solution was stored to keep out migrating waterfowl. And the list goes on.

An added side benefit at Beal resulted from the construction of a fish weir, which was made necessary because of rehabilitation taking place on Silver Bow Creek. The weir stopped the migration of other species of trout that might hybridize with the cutthroat, thus insuring genetic purity of the species in German Gulch.

"It's about the best in the state for wildlife mitigation," said Jim Jensen of the Montana Environmental Information Center in a 1991 article for *Trilogy* magazine by Mike Lapinski. "Beal Mountain is a good example that what's good for the environment can also be good for business."

"We take the view that environmental protection is good business, and are proud that [our] efforts have been recognized," said Eric Williams of Pegasus. "There are times when regulation can be onerous to industry while offering little or no protection of the environment. We have found this to be more of a function of requirements set at the bureaucratic level, which do not coincide with what is required statutorily.

"That said, I must stress Pegasus believes in prudent, reasonable regulation which allows responsible development of our natural resources and ensures environmental protection."

"From a historical perspective, there have been some pretty serious problems related to mining, but Pegasus has done some pretty neat things at Beal," commented Ray Tillman of Montana Resources and an active member of the George Grant Chapter of Trout Unlimited in Butte. "The industry is aware of public concern and that a bad operation can give it a black eye."

As an example of how far out in the nether reaches of left field the uninformed can be concerning mining, consider golf legend

Jack Nicklaus, who is designing a course near Anaconda at the Old Works Super Fund cleanup site (which is contaminated with extremely high levels of arsenic, lead, copper, zinc, and other metals). Nicklaus plans to cover this crud with a layer of topsoil and also to incorporate the remains of an old smelter into what promises to be a wildly different if not bizarre seventy-five-hundred-yard layout.

The goal according to Big Jack is to "remind you that you had mining here." That shouldn't be difficult, and visions of mad-as-a-hatter golfers tottering about in garish outfits flirts with the macabre, as does Nicklaus's plans for the sand traps.

He proposes using tons of black waste-slag for the traps to give the course a unique appearance.

"Heaven knows that nothing grows on it now," he said in an Associated Press story. "If we can grow grass in Hawaii on lava that we crushed, I don't see any reason that we can't do that here," Nicklaus added, concerning a proposal to mix the waste with topsoil for the fairways.

Maybe I'm missing something here, but the idea of standing in this lethal stuff or playing on top of it strikes me as a bit weird if not actually twisted. But hey! Where's the first tee and what's the course record?

From all of this it is obvious that the situation concerning mining and trout in Montana is in a state of flux. There are still many, many mining operations (especially smaller placer operations) that are seriously degrading the environment and destroying trout populations. But there are also examples like Pegasus at its Beal Mine that can point the way to the future, where possibly, just possibly, one of the state's most environmentally destructive industries can exist along with the trout and fly fishers and all the rest of us. I have strong doubts about this, as do others, though this pervading sense of doom has not stopped many from trying to save and improve the river's fishery.

As Becky Garland of the Big Blackfoot Chapter of Trout Unlimited said concerning mining in her part of the state, "If you have a healthy river valley from top of the basin to bottom of the basin, you have a healthy living and business climate and that's the reason we're all here in the first place."

Garland points out that fishing near Lincoln, where she operates her family store, is nothing like it was in the past, when she and her grandfather used to catch a "jillion, million brook trout" in headwater tributaries of the river. That fishery went belly-up when a tailings dam at the Mike Horse Dam broke in 1975, releasing tons of heavy metals into the upper drainage. The fishing has yet to recover, and trout as far downstream as sixty-five miles have tested positive for high concentrations of the deadly minerals.

"The proposed mining by Phelps-Dodge is moving along," said MDFWP fisheries biologist Don Peters. "When the wheels start rolling, people are pushed into the background, though they are meeting with us to try and smooth the waters. They're not stupid. Actually they're pretty smart concerning the approval process and they seem committed to an extensive mitigative approach.

"The spooky thing about the Blackfoot is that once you get something like this mine operational, it will be relatively easy to start up smaller sites when the big mine is played out. The small operations are often dirty, heavy polluters, and they are difficult to keep an eye on. The cultural impacts from the influx of miners on Lincoln will be tremendous, as will the impacts on wildlife and the fishery. Basically they will level a mountain in the process of mining the gold. Trees grow back eventually, sediment is flushed eventually, but the people that move in are usually permanent, and they will be the ones to start these small placer mines in the streambeds of the tributaries, which could mean real problems."

While Garland, other members of Trout Unlimited, concerned valley residents, guides, and outfitters, along with Peters and his peers, are less than optimistic about stopping the mine, they are proceeding full speed ahead with a number of stream-enchancement projects on Blackfoot tributaries that are already yielding results.

"TU has been a big mover, and one of them is writing grant requests, which is a tremendous help," said Peters. "They are also helping with landowner contacts and have mediated several situations. The majority of landowners have been extremely cooperative, but there are a few that will not deal with us. We do not have all the factors lined up—funding and contacts."

This funding includes a $200,000 challenge grant by the National Fish and Wildlife Fund, to be matched by $400,000, of which the Orvis Company has already contributed $113,161. Ducks Unlimited is also contributing money and labor to help restore riparian zones.

Much of the attention the Blackfoot is drawing comes from the movie *A River Runs Through It,* directed by Robert Redford and based on the Norman Maclean novella of the same title about a family growing up in the region earlier in the century. Proceeds from a special showing of the movie sponsored by the Big Blackfoot TU Chapter, the Clark Fork–Pend Oreille Coalition, and the Grizzly Hackle fly shop in Missoula also went for restoration work.

The only negative note to all of this was minor in nature but concerned an outdoor column in a local newspaper where the writer worried, with some justification, that the movie may bring too much attention to the Blackfoot. While this could happen, some fly fishers I spoke with felt that it was a bit odd and perhaps hypocritical for the writer in question to bring forth this concern after having discussed earlier in the piece the time he spent showing a production-company representative around the Blackfoot in search of film locations. You can't have things both ways, especially when trout streams are involved. The movie will no doubt bring "outsiders" into fly fishing and to the Blackfoot, but I think that the rivers in Montana need all of the supporters they can get. Compromise is everywhere these days, and fly fishing is no exception.

Some of the projects Peters mentioned concerned streams that once were excellent trout waters in their own right and may again be in the near future.

Rock Creek, a tributary of the North Fork not far from Ovando and located on private land, had an "overdesigned" culvert repaired, barriers removed, pools dug, woody debris for shelter added, and boulders placed in the streambed to improve flow. In

1991, brown trout redds were discovered in a formerly dewatered stretch with the possibility of hundreds of spawning sites appearing in the coming years. Peters adds that the same process is occurring with rainbows in the spring.

Nevada Spring Creek is considered one of the most critical spawning and rearing systems in the drainage, contributing as much as thirty percent of the flow to the main river. Until recently, the lower stretches heated to eighty degrees in the summer, eliminating any survival chances for trout. Work here has resulted in a "tremendous increase" in juvenile brown trout, according to Peters.

Other projects include fencing riparian areas to exclude grazing cattle along Elk Creek and working with Champion International to fix various culvert problems that prevent upstream movement by spawning trout. Enough of this action and the Blackfoot may soon return to the status of a topnotch trout stream.

While almost all of us would prefer to fish for trout instead of reading about or actually becoming involved in solving the numerous problems facing rivers like the Blackfoot, it is reassuring to know that this river is in so many good hands. Maybe Phelps-Dodge has a done deal with its gold mine, but they better run a clean operation. Too many people will accept nothing less.

There are many wonderful tributaries along the Blackfoot, and I remember one over by Ovando that produced some of the finest brook trout fishing I've found anywhere. Unfortunately, the ranchers that own the land surrounding the stream now deny access. Lynda and I found this out in a hurry one July evening. Still, they can't take my memories, which include one special outing in late May way back in the early seventies.

A couple of hipster friends and myself ignored classes at the University of Montana and rattled and bounced our way to the stream in an old Chevy pickup. We drank a few beers, smoked a touch of reefer (criminal behavior at its manifest worst), and talked away merrily about not much of anything. Seigel-Schwall was on the tape player.

The little creek wanders through dry sage-covered hills, alfalfa fields, and between willow-covered banks. Coming in at dusk, we only had time to catch a few small trout on nymphs before setting up camp and spending the evening talking around a small fire under a moon-bright sky as coyotes howled throughout the valley.

The next day was clear and soon hot, but the brook trout didn't mind. Hare's Ears, Elk Hair Caddis, Royal Wulffs, hoppers—the choice was not important. Fat, firm trout to eighteen inches came at almost every float. Once hooked, they dove for submerged roots, throbbing and shaking like crazy. We each probably caught a thousand trout. We kept a few for dinner and then split a Schmidt Sportsman twelve-pack while sitting on a low hill overlooking the stream and the feeding brookies. A pair of hawks worked a ridge line, gliding silently but efficiently far above. They dove and we heard the distant high-pitched screams of the victim rabbit. We three were happy predators and so, apparently, were the hawks.

I've been blessed with many good days on the stream, but this one is right at the top of the list—the colorful fish, the warm breeze filled with the smell of wildflowers that were blooming in the bright green grass, the distant timbered mountains, the blue sky and white cumulus clouds, the good friends. Damn hard to beat that combination, and I wish the ranchers would let me fish the water one more time. I'll ask again next summer. They were adamant in their refusal, but they didn't look like they'd shoot.

One place you can fish is the main river, which is accessible by highway and gravel county road for much of its serpentine length. The upper runs bend and arc through a gravel streamcourse guarded by timbered mountains. The river may be thirty to forty feet wide, at most. Flowing cold and deep blue, it has miles of long, swift glides and clear pools that brush up against undercut banks. There are browns and rainbows here, and cutthroat, too.

In the middle of the day in hopper season you can take fish steadily in the ten- to fourteen-inch range with noisy, attention-grabbing casts along the grassy, brushy banks. Watching the hoppers bang off dry land and then bounce downstream to be swiftly intercepted by eager trout is grand sport. 3-weights with weight-forward lines to slam the hoppers into their targets are perfect.

Later, as evening approaches, Elk Hairs in shades of gray (no Grateful Dead overtones intended) launched lightly upstream forty feet or so and dead-drifted take still more fish, mainly chubby golden-bellied browns that might reach fifteen inches on a good outing. Following the curvings of the river takes me quickly away from the road and everything else, and I could fish like this in the warm gathering darkness for a long, long time. The night holds the rich, fertile smell of the Blackfoot and the surrounding pines. Large caddis buzz about gently, stirring the still air. Stars are coming out and the coyotes are holding forth back in the hills. Bats are slicing up and down the river, and an owl deeply hoots somewhere behind me. The trout are rising steadily. They often come completely out of the water with the classic arched form that says clearly, "Damn! These bugs are good." This is perfect, and I'm glad I'm wading the river alone.

This upper piece of the river was visited by the Lewis and Clark caravan almost two hundred years ago as the party headed upstream, bound for buffalo country. Indians referred to the Big Blackfoot as *Cokahlahishkit*, or the "buffalo river road." The party had found little meat in the Bitterroots and was more or less desperate for buffalo and driven by hunger up the drainage toward Rogers Pass and what lay beyond on the windy plains. Lewis and Clark parted on July 4, 1806, with the former aiming up the Blackfoot to eventually explore the Marias River and the latter heading for the Yellowstone.

Lewis and his men camped about eight miles upriver from present-day Bonner, killing a couple of squirrels for specimens and then killing an antelope the next day near the mouth of the Clearwater River, which they named Werner's River, after a private in the group. They then passed the mouths of Cottonwood and Monture creeks and the North Fork, once called Salmon Trout Creek for the large bull trout that spawned in the stream's clean gravels. I imagine a few of these fish were netted or speared and cooked over a large fire that evening. Lewis also described a large crooked pond that might be present-day Brown's Lake. Mosquitoes drove the men crazy as they passed through the Blackfoot

*The Blackfoot River in the middle of April.*

Canyon west of Lincoln. The bugs are still holding their own, especially during a wet spring.

The party then trekked north up Alice Creek near the river's headwaters. Lewis wrote that in the drainage's high country, "deer are remarkably plenty and in good order" and that one of his men "wounded a moos deer" that was threatening the explorer's dog. From Roger's Pass the group spotted Square Butte, made famous in the paintings of Charles Russell. He also mentioned the "sighn of buffalo" when they camped at the headwaters of the Dearborn, just over the pass.

All of the above makes for interesting cocktail conversation, but the bottom line for any fly-fishing addict is working for trout. A bright, almost-full moon was well up in the east. Lynda and I finished off our steaks and wandered on toward the North Fork location where we'd seen a good rainbow working near shore and a deadfall earlier in the day.

The trout was there. We could see his head come out of the

water as he tagged the vulnerable caddis. The kype was visible, as was the silver-tipped suggestion of color along his gill plates. Things were bright out. Shadows from trees stretched dark and distinct across the water. You could read a book, maybe this one, in the light.

I was working somewhat carefully, and enough line was whizzing back and forth to cover the fish from a slight angle. The fly landed some feet ahead of the last rise with a slight curve in the leader. I could see the pattern's outline as it glided over the trout, which rose up and swallowed the thing. The fish streaked, leaped, splashed, and raised hell on the river with the feel of the hook-set. I almost fell into the water as I balanced on the downed tree.

The reel screeched madly (or was that Lynda?), and the rainbow jumped some more, not huge but strong, a happy sight in the cool light that illuminated the warm night. The trout dove and worked quickly to shore, then spooked at something, racing full-bore toward the middle of the North Fork. Slack ripped through the water, and the tippet popped when the line played out. The rainbow leaped clear of the water once, twice, three times — angry, elated, arrogant with its freedom? Who knows.

What the hell? There would be other fish. The night was young yet.

# JEFFERSON RIVER

Sometimes things do not work out and there are those trying moments when a bad situation turns dreadful. Such was the case on this early October trip in search of brown trout. The person accompanying me on the adventure and I failed to agree on anything—music, fly patterns, where to camp, how to fish—pick a topic, we managed to argue about it.

The scene gathered an ugly momentum when icy rains poured in from the southwest. Wet, cold, and surly, I pointed us toward Dillon and a dry motel room. I'd had enough and the visitor from the south and I soon parted ways. To be honest, I don't know how he got back home, and I don't care. Things were that bad. The only remorse I have is the three days I wasted, time the visitor spent whining in the truck (apparently the grilled pork tenderloin of the night before had been too much for his "finely tuned system"). Meanwhile, some classy trout streams east of Missoula fished as well as they ever have. The rivers were stylishly draped in glorious autumn splendor. Rainbows and browns were jumping to the Elk Hair Caddis rag on every other cast on the two streams I only briefly waded. Next year I would head off alone or ask Lynda if she wanted to go. No more wasted effort during the finest time of the year.

When I drove away from the motel parking lot in Dillon that morning, I experienced a sense of euphoria. I was on my own again and not responsible for anyone else. I felt as if I had escaped from a gruesome, insidious prison. Rolling merrily along and swiftly away from yesterday's miasma of ill will, I crossed the bridge spanning the Beaverhead at Twin Bridges and drove past the Blue Anchor Restaurant, a landmark of sorts for disoriented fly fishers. Somewhere between Hell Canyon Creek and Silver Star (population well less than one hundred and proud of it), I found myself in a perfect place beside the Jefferson River, tucked beneath some flaming gold cottonwoods out of sight of everyone except a stray raft of fly fishers that might come floating by.

I did not know if I was on private ranch land (no spray-painted-orange fence posts indicated that I was trespassing), state land, or somewhere in between. I gathered some fallen wood for a small evening fire, threw down my tarp and sleeping bag, set up a small folding chair, rigged up the 5-weight with a sinking tip and an olive Woolly Bugger, made a Bloody Mary, took a big sip, and thought, very loudly, Free at last. FREE AT LAST!

The weather was cold, blustery, cloudy. There was fresh snow on the sere bench land and low hills beyond the Jefferson below the Tobacco Root Mountains to the east, where still more of the stuff was piled. If it rained later, I'd sleep under the truck. I was too burned out to mess with the tent, especially in this breeze.

I pulled on my neoprene waders, laced up the wading shoes, finished the drink, and stepped into the river. Working cautiously up and across the river until I was close enough to reach the grassy bank, I launched the Bugger quartering upstream, allowed it to work beneath the undercut a little, and stripped it back in. Wham! First cast. A brown trout. I saw its yellow belly as the fish rolled near the surface before running downstream along the bank. The tippet was stout. I was not interested in fine art at the moment. I wanted to catch a couple of browns and hold them, let them go, and catch a few more. Basic fishing. There'd been enough crap on this trip already.

Plenty of fly line remained on the old banged-up Hardy Princess, which was my favorite reel. We'd caught a lot of trout together over the years, the Princess and I.

"Hold on a minute, Holt. You're turning maudlin on us here. How strong was that drink you made?"

*The Jefferson some miles below Twin Bridges in October.*
*This is prime water.*

"Sorry. I lost touch for a moment. I'll behave myself."

"Damn straight you will. Leave that sweetheart, me-and-old-Blue jive off the river; some of us are trying to fish."

Meanwhile, back at the ranch, the backing never came into play. The trout ran along the river bottom a few times, then came in. I pulled the fish to me by the leader, unhooking the Bugger after a moment's struggle. I'd forgotten to pinch down the barb. I watched the brown slide away with the current. Not twenty inches. Maybe sixteen. A good beginning.

I worked about two hundred yards of the bank, taking several more browns up to eighteen inches and one that was larger, a different class of fish: humped back, curled kype, thicker. A trout that had turned the corner from insects to preying on smaller fish full-time. These were the browns that hooked me. I'd rather catch these than any other trout (unless, as I've said before, I happen to be fishing for cutthroat or rainbows or goldens or brookies or bull trout and so on into sweet oblivion). Some thing about the secretive, mysterious, sharp-edged predatory ways of large browns draws me into the darker reaches of a river like no other species. Where casting to other trout is normally a pursuit of joy, of taking in all of the experience, the country, the weather, hunting browns is different. Watching the weather serves to indicate when to fish. Country is measured in terms of what a river offers in the way of shelter and food for the browns. Low light early in the morning or late in the evening translates not into flaming sunrises nor hypnotic campfires but rather into the hours of when big fish are knocking about. Most of us never see the truly big trout in a river. We are home reading or sleeping when the real predators come out to feed. If you want to touch big trout consistently, you have to be on the water in low light or darkness, an often frightening experience. Wading a big river negotiating strong current in blackout conditions is spooky, dangerous, and foolish. So what? I survived Beloit, Wisconsin. I've earned a few over-the-edge licks, and I've got life insurance. Even sedate fly fishers must take a few risks and hang out on whatever edge is available in order to blow away the cerebral cobwebs. Autumn brown trout fishing is essentially catch-and-release hunting. There is definitely an atavistic fervor to the pursuit. Once, after walking out of a river in early November, I caught a glimpse of myself in the side mirror as I removed my waders. It was the eyes that startled me. Wide, bulging a touch, the pupils pinned. Geez. I don't think I would have invited this version of me over to my house to meet the family. Apparently I'd been having too much fun.

The river was too deep and fast where I finished up, so I climbed the bank and walked back upstream, startling a whitetail buck and a couple of ring-necked pheasants in the process. Some cows mooed in a nearby pasture. At the truck the sun was out and the air had warmed to near fifty. I built a small charcoal fire in my miniature grill and cooked a two-pound rib eye to just past rare. The steak tasted tremendous. I opened a Pabst, plugged Robbie Robertson into the truck's tape player, and felt so damn good and relieved that I started laughing. Life was looking up, but then I was an easy sell at this point, a fly-fishing cement-head and proud of it.

The Jefferson flows for nearly eighty miles, first north, then almost dead east. The river boasts blue-blood lineage, being the product of the union, from east to west, of the Ruby, Beaverhead, and Big Hole rivers, all fair little trout streams in their own rights.

In many respects, the Jefferson River drainage bears only passing resemblance to the region explored by the Lewis and Clark expedition during the summer of 1805. Even the species of fish are different. Sure, there are still herds of mountain whitefish and a very few grayling in the headwaters of the Big Hole, but replacing the cutthroat are browns and rainbows, and brook trout in some of the tributaries. Small cutthroat also hold out in some of the mountain streams that run into the main river.

One major change is the Golden Sunlight Mine, north of the river between Whitehall and Cardwell at Bull Mountain. The operation is scalping the top of a mountain into a table-flat mixture of tailings and brute ugliness. If you want to see what the Phelps-Dodge mine at the headwaters of the Blackfoot will look like, come on down to Cardwell. Past mining activities have impacted a tributary of the Jefferson called the Boulder River, along with a number of its feeder streams. This watershed is not expected to return to fishing form in my lifetime or yours, or my children's either, for that matter. The Boulder River itself has a nice run of browns up from the Jefferson for several airline miles upstream to a diversion dam. The season closes September 30 to protect the trout.

Present-day Three Forks is an area of open cattle country, irrigated alfalfa fields, and diminishing wild grasslands. When Clark arrived, after temporarily separating from Lewis, the area abounded in otter, beaver, deer, even elk and antelope. Today, those animals are present, especially the deer, but much of the country has been tamed. Clark chose the westernmost of the three forks that today are known as the Gallatin, Madison, and Jefferson because the river appeared to cut into the mountains sooner than the other two streams to the east.

Today, I-90 and various state roads cross the river. The water here has twelve- to fifteen-inch browns, but the numbers are not as good as they are farther upstream. Cottonwoods line the banks. Waterfowl make extensive use of the swampy bottoms and braided main and side channels. U.S. 10 parallels the stream on the north, and you can drive along through the gently rolling hills of the now agrarian valley before entering a narrow, steeply walled canyon that has a gloomy appearance in low light due in part to the dark gray color of the rock. Lewis and Clark Caverns State Park is located on the north side of the Jefferson.

This constricted stretch begins near Sappington Bridge and runs for about a dozen miles of riffle and long deep-pool water up to La Hood. Fish numbers are low here, but the trout may average larger than anywhere else on the river, especially below the outlet of the South Boulder River by the London Hills. Drys in the evening and streamers worked down low all of the time take mainly browns, along with some rainbows. Trains rumble by on tracks that follow the river from both sides. This is kind of an eerie place to fish, but I've taken some nice, sociable browns on Blue-Winged Olives before runoff and in the fall, along with plenty of slurping, sucking, slobbering whitefish. The browns tend to hold farther out, feeding in the faster water along the faintly visible seams of current. This is also nice water to probe with large, heavily weighted sculpin patterns attached to Hi-D Sink-Tips. Freewheeling, carefree work that requires some concentration and caution. A weighted streamer traveling at one hundred miles an hour hurts, after you come to. A friend nailed himself in the head with one of these, and I could hear the telltale bone-and-metal *clunk,* even though I was standing well upstream. He actually staggered and weaved as he left the stream. You really have to admit that fly fishing can be darn good sport at times.

"What in the hell is going on? God, my head hurts."

"Take some aspirin."

"Is the twenty-gauge still behind the seat?"

Or something along these lines.

There are fishing accesses, some improved camping spots, and rough paths down to the water that can be reached along the assortment of paved and unpaved roads and highways. One of the best accesses, which is quite popular locally, is at Cardwell. The site itself is unsightly. Outhouses. A rutted dirt parking lot. Cans and cigarette butts scattered all over the place. But the fishing is good even though the water is often a murky olive color from irrigation water return and nutrient influx from multiple sources. There are steady hatches of both caddis and mayflies. Streamers and larger nymphs also produce.

Above Cardwell, the Jefferson meanders through cottonwood-lined banks past ranch country, and much of the land is posted. The Highland Mountains hold forth in the west. According to MDFWP biologist Bruce Rehwinkel, the fishery is ninety percent browns and ten percent rainbows below Kountz Bridge a few miles southeast of Whitehall and the deadly Piedmont Swamp that figures prominently in local bar legend. Above the bridge, the figure drops to eighty percent browns and twenty percent rainbows. There are loads of whitefish throughout the drainage. There are also a number of temporary tractor-spawned gravel irrigation diversions that partially block the flow of the Jefferson and provide ideal spawning habitat for carp and suckers. Overall, the browns probably run around fourteen or fifteen inches, with some that are much rarer and harder to catch coming in at several pounds.

When Clark reached the main forks of the Jefferson, he and his party followed his scout's tracks up a willow-choked, beaver-riddled fork of the Jefferson. At night they camped on ground that was so swampy they were forced to build willow nests to stay out of the muck. There were probably a couple of mosquitoes flitting around that evening, also. They eventually worked past the Ruby, which they named Philanthropy, and the Big Hole, which they called Wisdom. The Jefferson above the forks was named after Beaverhead Rock, easily discernible today, originally described by the Shoshone. They proceeded up to present-day Horse Prairie Creek. Eventually they worked their way to Lemhi Pass down into the Bitterroot and on to the Clark Fork and the Pacific.

The geology of the drainage contributes directly to much of the river's present problems. Bull Mountain is composed mostly of a volcanic rock known as andesite that erupted from the magma of the Boulder batholith before it crystallized. The rock lies on a base of tightly folded belt and Paleozoic sedimentary rock: For a frame of reference, cast back anywhere from 200 million to more than a billion years ago. The Golden Sunlight Mine started up with the discovery of demon gold in 1892 and produced on an irregular basis according to the fluctuating price of the metal until 1982, when the operation went crazy as an open-pit monstrosity. As long as there is gold fever, men will hammer away at the mountain. Someday they could perhaps build a golf course on the site, but don't breathe a word of this to Jack Nicklaus, or Arnie, either.

The north end of the Jefferson Valley is comprised of basin fill sediment as much as four thousand feet thick that piled up several million years ago during a period of damp tropical climate. Doherty Mountain north of I-90 is marked by striking white cliffs consisting of Cambrian limestone. In the south there are yellowish Precambrian sandstones that trend toward the LaHood formation that is exposed in the Jefferson Canyon. The weathered green strips visible in the road cuts are andesite.

The Precambrian LaHood formation reveals that the dark gray rock is studded with chunks of metamorphic and igneous rocks set in dark green mudstone that was deposited in a series of mud flows millions of years ago. This formation marks the southern margin of the Precambrian belt and is called the Willow Creek fault. Once again we are back to dealing in terms of billion-year segments of time.

The Tobacco Root Mountains dominate the valley, rising abruptly from the valley to more than ten thousand feet. The glaciated peaks were carved from a massive granite batholith that pushed through the Precambrian basement 70 million years ago. Mining occurs on a smaller and infrequent basis in these mountains.

The mineral deposits that are present in large quantities in all of these formations and structures spawned a prolonged and sometimes intense mining activity that in turn created millions of tons of mining tailings and other pollutants like cyanide that have drastically limited the area's fishing potential. Some of the streams in the Boulder River have at most only a few stunted, sickly trout. The possibilities in this pretty watershed are depressing to contemplate, once again because they will never be realized while I'm around. Cleanup would be costly, to put things mildly.

"Any time you have a cyanide leaching operation you have the potential for problems, but, generally speaking, I think we are getting the message out," says Rehwinkel. "On another front we are seeing lots of guys returning fish back to the river, returning those genes back into the pool. Catch-and-release coupled with habitat restoration is also helping the rainbow population."

With all of the topnotch water pouring into the Jefferson, one would think that this might be the best brown trout river in the world. It is not. The fishing can be good, but the numbers of catchable trout are not what they should be. According to Rehwinkel there are anywhere between two hundred and six hundred browns per mile in the lower river and a few more in the smaller upper stretches.

"I have a strong feeling that the Jefferson is under-recruited due in part to incubation problems for the rainbows and a sediment problem with the browns," comments the biologist. "There probably should be twice as many brown trout. The river has dried up before and this devastates trout in the zero to one age classes. Unfortunately, we're caught in between promoting the Jefferson to develop a constituency that will protect and improve the resource and trying to keep the river anonymous. Let's just say there are no easy solutions."

While the mean flow in September, after irrigation season concludes, is in the 1,400 cfs range at Three Forks, there are times when summer flows plummet as low as they did during the 1988 drought, when they bottomed out at well less than 100 cfs. Large sections of stream channel went bone dry under an unrelenting sun and the never-ending irrigation demands of area ranchers. This combination is having a severe impact on rivers all around Montana, particularly east of the Continental Divide. And as Rehwinkel said, there are no easy solutions. The Jefferson is a classic example of the in-stream flow problems facing the West.

Battles over who owns the water in the West will be one of the significant environmental issues in the coming decades, greater than logging, mining, or even development. Without water there will be no development. And states downstream of flows in the Rockies and other parts of the West are clamoring for their share of water. Complicated legal battles that will make tying a Bimini Twist on acid seem straightforward are looming on the parched horizon. All of this litigation will have profound effects on trout streams. Some may even be sucked permanently dry in order to satisfy our insatiable need for water.

The way the situation concerning in-stream flows stands right now in Montana, there is not much that can be done to rectify the harmful situations created in the past. Some hope is seen for the future, though progress will be extremely slow in coming.

Ranching and the right to divert river water to irrigate fields of alfalfa and other crops necessary for raising cattle goes back to the 1860s. Many prior appropriations are well over a century old. Impacts from these demands affect trout populations throughout the West. During drought years, and these are becoming the rule rather than the exception as regional weather patterns seem to be moving into a dry cycle, a rancher's diversion of a river's water can stress a population of fish in lethal measures or can dry up a river entirely, as happened on the Jefferson, Big Hole, parts of the Sun, and numerous other trout streams in 1988, and to a lesser extent succeeding irrigation seasons.

"This is a visceral issue, a difficult one to break through on," says Helena-based Trout Unlimited member and environmental attorney Stan Bradshaw. "The state supreme court has ruled that water rights are considered property rights, but pre-1973 water rights cannot be transferred to in-stream flows. This needs to be changed. I don't mind the idea of paying some rancher for his water, but the way the system is now, we can't do this. And some ranchers are so paranoid concerning change, even benign change, it is frightening."

What Bradshaw is getting at is that, for example, if a rancher decides for whatever reason that he no longer requires or desires to use his water allocation, he is unable to sell or transfer this water to the state or a conservation group to benefit a recreational use such as fly fishing. He can sell the water to another rancher or to someone who needs the liquid to operate a highly polluting placer mining operation, or to a rural electrical coop for power generation.

"I'm not as pessimistic as some people out there," adds Bradshaw. "East of the Divide we have some protection through junior water rights. We need to change the regulatory and legal infrastructure. I believe that we will have more meaningful protection in the future."

The junior water rights Bradshaw referred to are any recognized claims on water allocated after other rights. They do not supersede rights from the 1860s, but they do have precedence over any claims made by, say, a subdivision developer in the coming years. They are at least some measure of protection for a trout stream.

"First in time, first in right," says Liter Spence, MDFWP Water Resources Supervisor. "They [usually ranchers] are entitled to use the water as they see fit. If they dry up a trout stream, that's too bad as long as the use is deemed beneficial. In the old days they could dig a ditch and divert the water whenever they saw fit to do so. Things have changed some since then."

Beneficial use covers a broad spectrum of activities such as irrigation, watering cattle, and mining. Spence explained that Murphy Rights, legislation introduced by a state congressman of the same name, were approved for twelve drainages in the sixties. This was a tentative first step that protected these streams from claims coming after 1971 or the priority date. The rights do not supersede previous claims. The dozen streams are: The Flathead and its three forks (North, Middle, and South), Madison, Gallatin, Smith, Missouri, Rock Creek, Blackfoot, Yellowstone, and Big Spring Creek.

The Water Use Act of 1973 essentially reaffirmed Murphy Rights, affirming that the state owns the water and that people have a right to the water, but once again prior appropriations were not subordinated. As noted, progress moves at its own casual pace in water law.

"This is obvious, but there are three components for a trout stream," says Spence. "You need a stream channel compatible with the needs of the fish, you need good water quality, and you need a sufficient quantity of water. Trout need a physical home where they can do their thing."

A study being conducted by Chris Clancy, a biologist for the MDFWP, on the Bitterroot River reaffirms the idea that diverting water for irrigation has a deleterious effect on trout. "The rainbow trout adults migrate from the Bitterroot River in March, April, and May and spawn in these streams," says Clancy. "Usually about the beginning of July, the fry begin to migrate back toward the river. At this time we set traps in three locations in each stream. We set one trap upstream of the ditch, one in the ditch, and one downstream of the ditch."

The idea according to Clancy is that the upstream trap quantifies how many fry are potentially produced. The middle trap measures how many are lost in the ditch, and the downstream trap quantifies how many fry make it past the ditch. In theory, the downstream trap and the ditch trap numbers should equal the numbers obtained from the upstream trap. (There are minor variations due in part to differences in stream flow and the amount of water passing through the trap.)

As an example, on Big Creek during 1991, 3,270 fry were calculated to be drifting upstream, with 1,023 going down the ditch and 2,221 making it downstream. That leaves twenty-six unaccounted for, or less than two percent. The same held true for similar work done on Blodgett Creek.

"The whole upshot is that in two years of sampling, fifteen to thirty percent of the fry were lost in the Big Creek trap and twenty to forty percent were lost into the Blodgett Creek ditch," says Clancy, who cautioned that the study is ongoing and more data is needed before making any definitive conclusions.

It would appear that not only does irrigation diversion harm trout habitat, it also sucks young-of-the-year trout away from the stream and into a diversion ditch, never to be heard from again.

"We have a hard time keeping water in the rivers," says Spence. "All we can do is defend the rights we have now."

The Board of Natural Resources and Conservation also granted in-stream flows on the Yellowstone in 1978, and as of 1992, 250 streams in the Missouri Basin above Fort Peck Dam received similar protection. Once again, these do not supersede previous priority dates but may protect against future claims.

Spence explained that there are a number of permits processed that appear to be junior to MDFWP's rights in the basin, but that the board can subordinate these rights. So the status of countless claims is still high and dry.

"We still have to deal with a number of permits and we do not know if the board will handle these separately or all at once," said Spence. "This could in effect move our priority date back to 1992. We like to look at this for the future, but we must put our rights in use immediately in order to establish our right to use the water. And sometime in the future there will probably be a court case among the Missouri Basin states. Just because you live upstream does not mean that you have rights to the water."

This refers in part to a state supreme court ruling in 1992 that upheld a state law that requires Montanans to claim their water rights by 1982 based on a deadline passed in 1979 by the state legislature. Remember, things move slowly when water is the issue. Over 200,000 claims were filed before the deadline, and another 3,242 were filed after the closing date. There is a thirty-year period for implementing these rights. Again, think *slow*. The court ruled that late filers effectively surrendered their claims by missing the deadline.

Spence is also referring to the fact that states downstream from Montana are demanding sufficient water releases from Fort Peck and other storage units to maintain stream levels adequate for barge traffic. Tremendous impacts could be felt by fly fishers along the upper Missouri if increased releases are ordered in the future.

There has been some solid progress made with ranchers and the water conservation districts they belong to according to Spence, especially in the Big Hole and to a lesser extent on the Jefferson. The MDFWP is trying to protect the last remaining original river-dwelling population of grayling in the state, and the cooperation of area ranchers is crucial to a successful effort.

"We've been working on the Missouri above Canyon Ferry to keep water in streams for spawning rainbows—for the eggs, emerging fry, and for downstream migration," reports Spence. "We helped the Broadwater-Missouri Ditch Company utilize their water more efficiently with an improved system. The company was cooperative and a big help. We have already seen an improvement in recruitment levels in the involved streams.

"This is a transitional period concerning in-stream flows, with emphasis shifting some to new uses like fishing and other recreational uses. This all is going to take time, and we won't get anywhere if we pit one group against another."

Other positive signs include increased interest in a water lease bill passed by the 1989 state legislature that allows the MDFWP to lease water rights for preservation of critical in-stream flows. The program provides money to water users for not diverting their water during critical months or years, but allows them to use the water at other times. The department has already checked out leasing potential on dozens of stretches of impacted streams.

State officials are also trying to purchase water from Painted Rocks Lake, located above the West Fork of the Bitterroot River, in order to provide more water to protect invertebrates and trout during irrigation season.

An ad hoc group called Montana River Watch was formed in 1992 to monitor calls concerning stream-flow problems. The complaints that year ranged from diversions to dry streambeds to too many fishermen to a pigpen in Belt Creek. Goals and objectives of the group were to achieve awareness and recognition of instream flow problems and to establish a core support group.

River Watch is also concerned that implementation of the Montana Streambed Preservation Act is in the hands of conservation district supervisors with little representation by conservation groups, that emergency provisions allow permits to be approved without due process, and that the act has "no teeth," allowing conservation districts to administer the law with little oversight.

"Faced with new needs, we must increase our support to activities that will help us understand and mitigate the pressures of coming years," said Montana Trout Foundation president Bob Buzzas. The group was responsible for forming River Watch. "It's time to look ten, twenty, thirty years and more downstream. We need visionary stewards, today. There exists an opportunity to educate the agricultural community on water transfer rights.

"Guys are building structures [diversions] up and down the river. These often violate turbidity standards, but no one is cited for anything. All we're trying to point out is that Montana's Streambed Preservation Act is worthless."

MDFWP biologist Ron Spoon has been caught in the middle of the controversy. He has seen firsthand the stress put on fish in the Jefferson when flows drop to 20 or 30 cfs for as long as a month in certain parts of the river. He says that most of the fish are concentrated in pools, that the low flows chronically crop off young fish, and that larger trout are able to hang on because the small amount of flow in the stream comes from cooler upwelling groundwater. One recent diversion of gravel, rock, and dirt spanned most of the Jefferson.

"When the diversion first happened, the publicity was great. It focused a lot of attention on the problem and helped get people involved," says Spoon. "But some folks have really continued to press on with this backing the ditch company into a corner. They are now in a defensive posture. They are angry and lashing out and they don't know what people want from them. The situation is basically a mess right now. I understand both sides of the issue, but polarizing people is not the answer. I do know that this is going to be fixed, probably by 1994."

So the bottom line as far as in-stream flows are concerned on the Jefferson and other western trout streams is that prior water rights cannot be subordinated. Junior rights are needed to protect rivers from future demands by developers, mining, and the like; and the only concrete changes will come from changing law to allow the transfer of water rights to recreational users and by working hand in hand with ranchers and their conservation districts.

The Jefferson was the river where I first began to catch browns with any consistency over twenty years ago. The drive to the water was less than three hours from my rent-a-dump in Missoula. These were years predating my current Woolly Bugger period. The Jefferson is primarily a streamer river for me and many other fly fishers, but back in those fun-filled days of hipsterness I pretty much limited myself to patterns like Royal Wulffs, Adamses, and Elk Hairs. The amazing thing was that these basics took browns during the dog days of summer when water levels were low and temperatures were up, and they still do almost everywhere. True, the best times were early in the day before the heat and light, or toward dusk as the day began to cool off.

Brown trout in this river resemble the Loch Leven to some degree in that the red spotting and bright golden yellow bellies found in trout of the Madison or the Bitterroot, for example, are not as apparent. These fish are more subdued in color, with broader expanses of silver and greater areas of black spotting, along with deep flanks. In many respects they look like the lake-dwelling browns who could be their ancestors.

I always thought that a brown trout was a brown trout, but cursory research reveals browns are essentially *Salmo trutta* with subspecies (though these classifications are in a constant state of flux, as are those of most salmonid species, including rainbows and their clan, which were once considered *Salmo* but are now classified as *Oncorhynchus* because their behavior more closely resembles that of Pacific salmon than of Atlantic salmon), including the Black Sea trout, Caspian trout, North African trout (which I've taken on occasion, not surprisingly in Morocco), and the Aral trout or possibly Turkish "Allah Bailik" or god's fish. There are several species resembling browns, which include the Sevan trout of Armenia, the softmouth of Yugoslavia that has a mouth resembling a sucker's, the Italian Garda trout, the Ohrid from Yugoslavia, and yet another Yugoslavian species, the marble trout, which may reach forty pounds, is extremely predacious and is found only in Dalmatian rivers holding plenty of forage fish. In the early seventies I intended to try and catch these marble fish but was turned away at the border. The guard, who was into black leather gloves, pants, boots, and helmet, fashionably accentuated with black wrap-a-round sunglasses (the black-on-black look made so popular by the Velvet Underground in the sixties), told me the country was closed on account of plague and to head my USA act elsewhere. I took his generous advice and flew to Casablanca, then struck intrepidly off into the Atlas Mountains, where I found some brown trout swimming in small stretches of a few spring creeks in the hills some miles above scenic downtown Agadir, but that is truly another story, riddled with Berber hashish salesmen, sweet mint tea, and splattered tomatoes. One hopes that the Moroccan authorities have short memories.

The first browns in North America were introduced by a New York fish culturist named Fred Mather, who managed with some difficulty to import eighty thousand eggs from the Black Forest of Germany with the assistance of Baron von Behr, president of the German Fishery Association way back in 1883. The initial

*A Jefferson Loch Leven taken in October.*

introduction in this country of Scotland's Loch Leven strain occurred in 1885 with a shipment of 100,000 eggs from Stirlingshire. The von Behr trout are known as *Salmo fario,* and the Loch Leven variety is *Salmo levenensis.* Using Latin is so exciting.

In 1897, the Michigan Conservation Commission considered the brown "inferior in every respect to the brook or rainbow." Back in those olden days, Montana fisheries officials called the brown "a good fish, but the average angler is not skilled enough to catch it." Because browns do feed aggressively on surface insects, it is responsible for much of the angling lore and history in this country, and the species eventually received wide-ranging acceptance.

Whatever species or strain, the browns of the Jefferson will rise to drys, though the best fish are often taken on streamers in the fall. Tim Tollett of Frontier Anglers prefers large streamers and wet-fly patterns in autumn to take browns that he says average a little over two pounds, with three- and four-pound fish not uncommon. He prefers a pattern of his own design called Tim's

Cockyabully, which resembles a Bugger to some extent but has a weighted, tapered body with palmered grizzly hackle and a grizzly tail.

"Hatches on the river are not as significant as on other quality streams in the state due in large part to dewatering and the inherent damage to invertebrate habitat," says Ron Spoon. "There are a variety of caddis hatches from April into October, including *Baetis* in the spring and fall."

Caddis hatches to look for, though they do not approach the prolific activity on the nearby Madison or the Gallatin, are: greenish brown grannom in #12–14 beginning in late April and running into May; a yellowish brown spotted sedge, #10–14, from mid-May through July; the olive brown great gray spotted sedge, #6–8, in June and July; green sedge, #12–14, for most of the summer on into September with patterns imitating the peeking caddis nymph, and Hare's Ears, which are always good selections; and a ginger longhorn sedge, #12–14 in the summer. These are all productive patterns, but the bugs never come off the Jefferson with anything approaching the predictability of emergences on the Madison, at least not in my experience. I tend to fall back on my box of Elk Hairs in various shades and sizes to match the hatch.

There are a number of mayflies that appear throughout the year, and they include blue-winged olives (both *Baetis tricaudatus* and *parvus*) in #18–20 in the spring and during the fall. This is a productive pattern anywhere, but as mentioned earlier, the whitefish also love this fly. Browns can be taken, though irregularly, amid the pods of slurping whitefish, but working out toward the faster stretches of the river takes better trout.

The Western Black Quill can be significant, especially along the upper stretches where faster water is found from June through July, in #12 with a purplish black body and gray wing. Yellow-olive pale morning duns are more of a spring creek hatch, but there is some emergence along the upper stretches from Twin Bridges to Parsons Bridge, notably near the entrance of cold-water tributaries, such as they are. Access on the upper river is spotty, and floating covers the water with a certain ease and illusion of elegance. Look for #16–18 in the summer after runoff, with duns coming off the water about 10:00 A.M. and spinner falls occurring in the morning and at dusk. During cool, cloudy days of early summer, the western green drake, #10–12, appears with spinner falls early in the day and duns emerging in late morning. The same holds true for the small western green drake in #14.

Brown drakes are seen in slower sections of the river in June and July in #12, with duns emerging before dusk and spinners falling a bit later. Another hatch common to the region but not usually seen on the Jefferson is the gray drake, #10–12, in mid-June emerging in late morning into the afternoon. Flavs (*Ephemer-ella flavilinea*) are a June and July mayfly that comes off during cool, moist afternoons in #14–16. Because of the amount of slow water on the Jefferson, I often look for speckled-wing spinners (*Callibaetis nigritus*) in July and August in a gray #14–16. This can be a surprisingly good hatch on a number of slower stretches. Finally, tricos from late July into September can tempt some large trout, including the infrequent Jefferson rainbow in a #20–22 with a black body and a white Z-lon wing to imitate the spinner. Look for the duns at first light and the spinners early in the morning. Light tippets and frequent break-offs are the rule with these bugs.

Because the streambed has been degraded from silt and pollution, the once-prolific hatches of stoneflies have dwindled into virtual insignificance. Things like Yellow Sallys and Sofa Pillows ride nicely on the water but are not usually productive. Hoppers along the grassy banks are excellent choices once the runoff drops and the weather warms, especially near hay fields and on breezy days when a rancher is cutting his crop. This can be wildly exciting action. Reddish brown ants in #14–16 also work, and I suspect a small rattlesnake tie of six inches or so would turn some nice trout along some stretches of the river.

Other streamer or big-nymph patterns include the Yuk Bug; Girdle Bug; white, black, or yellow Marabou Muddlers; Zonkers; Princes; and Bitch Creeks. Royal Trudes can be nice prospecting patterns at these times.

The Jefferson has its problems, difficulties that limit the amount of insect life and in turn the predictability of the hatches, but the bugs are there. Most skilled fly fishers think streamers when they turn to this river, but talking with those who fish the river dozens of times a season has made me aware of the surface activity that is perhaps the most exciting of all trout fishing. For the Jefferson and most other streams, a dropper tied in using the extended tag of a blood knot connection on the tippet can prove doubly effective. With caddis I use a dry (of course it's an Elk Hair most of the time) on the dropper and an emerger on the point that may be a Serendipity, a Z-lon Emerger, a Hare's Ear, or one of my favorites, an Olive Sparkle Pupa. Tim Tollett turned me on to this Gary LaFontaine pattern on the Beaverhead one hot August day, and I've caught big fish with it on a number of streams. Soft hackles are also fine choices. The dry fly actually serves as a form of indicator (never, *never* say "bobber," or you will be mercilessly flogged with cane rods by hordes of tweedy fly fishers that descend from out of nowhere; just be sure to remember that using egg and fish patterns is for the most part acceptable) for when a fish takes the emerger.

The wind was gone and so was Robbie Robertson. I rebuilt the charcoal fire and burned a Cornish game hen (you get hungry playing outside all day) that was basted with extra virgin olive oil, crushed garlic, and ground black pepper. This went quite well with some Brie on unsalted rye crackers and a bottle of Merlot I'd stashed far from the prying attentions of the long-gone visitor from the south. Feeling sated and quite happy, I wadered up, as they say in the Westerns, and worked my way out into the Jefferson, now turned glassy quiet with only a few ripples of current breaking the mood. I stood there puffing on a cheap oscuro-wrappered cigar thrown together by someone in Connecticut as I waited for some trout to show themselves. And pretty soon they did. Several large noses appeared out in the center of the river, upstream and perhaps forty feet away.

Because my approach to casting has never been described as "delicate," or for that matter "graceful," "accurate," or "technically correct," I was using a 3-weight and its delicate line to try and soften the impact of my presentations. After quickly working enough line out to cover the lower of the risers, I quartered the cast above the fish and managed to impart a touch of fade to the leader with a turn of my wrist. The Olive bore in on the trout, which went head up and tail down with the take, setting the hook on its own and running across and downstream immediately. Smoke from the cigar swirled around my head as I pivoted on my left heel and watched the proceedings like a lord of the manor taking in his expansive, manicured grounds while sipping cognac after a fine dinner.

The brown stopped somewhere below me and shook its head, causing the line to razor the river's surface in tight, rapid strokes. I still had done nothing but turn and watch the action. Lifting the rod slightly sent the trout off on another short run, and some gentle persuasion put line back on the reel. Rod in the right hand, cigar in the left, I thought, What a difference a day can make, and the fish ran once more, though he seemed to be tiring.

Clamping the stinking, smoking stogie between my teeth, I reeled the brown, who now offered only token resistance, to me. The fish was thick, wide, and without red spots again. Probably not twenty inches. I passed on marking him against the rod, preferring to exaggerate his size in my mind's eye. The big guy swam off in the slightly murky green water and I took a large puff on the cigar, sending clouds of acrid smoke into the atmosphere. The other two browns were still working above me, no doubt awaiting my next delicate offering.

Let them wait. There was plenty of time left burning in the day. Feeling the current work past my legs, staring off into the Tobacco Roots, listening to the cottonwood leaves rustle in the soft breeze took precedence. The browns kept on sipping and I kept on standing there watching them.

# TONGUE RIVER

*T*he sage grouse was excellent grilled over glowing coals and smoking mesquite chips. I'd shot the bird as it lumbered up into the air on a sage flat high above the river. The grouse was one among dozens (the smallest and I hoped youngest, for reasons of flavor and tenderness, that I could spot quickly) that broke free in the chill air. I dropped the bird quickly, bringing the twenty-gauge to bear and swinging slightly through the shot before the grouse could power off downwind. After cleaning the four-pound bird and keeping some feathers for PMDs (there were bunches of them ideally shaded yellowish blue-tan), I walked up to the wide, churning stretch below the dam that restrained the held-back Tongue River Reservoir. Water poured through a large tunnel in the center of the impoundment with a steady roar. This was a decidedly weird place to fish for brown trout. So what's new?

I flung a solder-wire-weighted sculpin with a sinking tip line far out into the plunge pool; my quick stripping retrieves turned up a sauger, a couple of tags from unidentified submerged objects, and no brown trout. After an hour I gave up and walked back to camp, dodging dried cow pies as I went. The "campground" was empty as the place always was, but there was litter scattered about and I spent another hour picking the crud up, righteous indignation swelling in my chest. Garbage, even here in the middle of nowhere. Humans are slobs all too often and there's too damn many of us. I hope the lemming factor will kick in soon.

The wild, slightly sage-flavored meat and a baked potato loaded with butter, sour cream, and chives overcame a slight feeling of depression. I've fished the river for several years now, spurred by rumors from some of my diehard fly-fishing friends who had passed on their hopes concerning the possibility of gamefish in this lost-in-the-ozone piece of southeastern Montana just a six-pack north of Sheridan, Wyoming. Indeed, the rumors had proved modestly true. There were browns in the Tongue River, not many, but a few that might run several pounds, and I wanted to catch one more this year. My friend John Talia and I were over here in coulee-and-bluff country in the spring and we managed to catch a couple more sauger and two browns of less than twenty inches. These on black Woolly Buggers in the dark. This was in late April, with the land already parched. Ninety-degree temperatures fried small rattlesnakes as they lay comatose in the dusty-salmon roads. Many were smashed flat by the infrequent passing pickup way out here in empty coal and ranch country. Their carcasses provided graphic testimony to the fact that reptiles along with insects and arachnids far outnumber salmonids along the Tongue, as well they should.

The dinner was excellent and so was the Honduran cigar I was puffing on in the still air of an October evening. A Cuban Cohiba Robusto would have been that much better, but at four-hundred-dollars-plus a box they were out of my league, for now. As I scanned the moving water looking for feeding browns next to current edges or along the undercut grassy banks, the sense of being completely alone at the ends of the earth was overpowering. Chunky mule deer picked their way along an ochre-and-buff hill marked with a thick seam of jet black coal. The wild grasses were dead brown and the sage was dusky gray.

A tremendous squawking, quacking racket erupted in the bare cottonwood behind me. Looking up, I saw a most incongruous sight. A large duck, unidentifiable in the fading light, was swinging back and forth flapping its wings as it frantically tried to free itself from a couple of limbs where it had somehow managed to wedge its throat. The frightened duck spun around on the axis of its neck, finally breaking free just short of snapping its spine, I'm sure. The bird staggered off in wobbly flight over the ridge with the browsing mule deer.

Flicking the ash from my cigar, I noticed two small, dark brown caddis crawling on my hand, size 18 or less. Turning back to the water, I saw a large brown leap free of the river in a perfect arc and then slip back into the water. The fish appeared and then vanished so quickly I wondered if it had been real. Running and stumbling over downed limbs and brush and through crackling piles of dry leaves, I raced to the 8-weight, tore off the sculpin, reeled in the sinking tip, changed to a floating 7, hastily tied in some fresh 5X tippet, and then spun on a brown Elk Hair of the appropriate size.

Working quickly but somewhat quietly downstream of where the brown had shown itself, I waded out into the shallow rushing water and cast, angling upstream toward the bank. I lost contact with the fly but clearly saw the big head come up to suck the bug in. I set the hook by lifting the rod, and the trout tore off down and across stream with the line knifing the water and the reel spinning away. The fish was a nice one—I could tell from the size of the swirl as it boiled the water seventy feet away. The brown ran again, pulling still more line from the reel, and I stumbled over small rocks and gravel as I splashed along in the gathering dark. Large shapes made big vees in the water as they swam away from me. The brown stopped, held, and I could force it some while gaining twenty feet or so of line before the fish buzzed off toward Miles City. I tried to keep pace.

The brown led this clumsy dance for a few more minutes with line steadily coming back to the reel. Then I was on top of the trout as it held in the still water near shore. This was a brown over twenty inches, maybe a twenty-two, but even in the low light the difference between this fish and those of the Jefferson was obvious. The fish was wide yet still sleek and menacing, like a Trident submarine, and the colors were really brown, dark brown. The belly glistened yellow brown and the black spots were hard to make out. The few crimson marks seemed to glow in the last of the dying light.

*Working rising carp on the Tongue.*

This was why I was here. The elusive, rare, seldom-caught Greater North American Tongue River Brown Trout that figures prominently in my febrile imagination. You can have the permit and the bones and the New Zealand rainbows and the Norwegian Atlantic salmon. I'd rather drive over to this water-starved country packed with cactus, black widows, brown recluses, chiggers, big biting flies, and all kinds of snakes and fish for these few browns. The nearest gas station or motel was more than an hour's worth of serious driving away from my campsite. Way out here with the grouse and the muley bucks and the turkeys I could misbehave all I wanted. Drink way too much, stay up past the late-night news, and howl with the wild dogs. This was designer terrain for a full-bore recluse. To be honest, the browns were an excuse to drive the almost seven hundred miles down from Whitefish to play in this arid landscape. The knowledge that the nearest yupster was several hours away was reassuring, like escaping a really dull dinner party full of people I hardly know.

I worked back upriver and launched the fly slightly inside a band of current that bulged and rippled near the middle of the Tongue. Nothing. I cast again. Nothing. The light was about gone and the climbing moon was muted by a bank of feathery clouds riding in on the night wind. Cast again. The fly was lost from view. Silver light splashed off a swirl of a rising fish and I struck. Too damn hard. The trout broke free and jumped like a rodeo mustang, back bent into a signature curve as the fish leaped above the river. I tied on another Elk Hair in the blackness, but I'd had my chances and life was good and some Jack Daniels and another strong cigar while rocking from foot to foot standing over a deadwood fire would be all right, too.

Tongue River country is an acquired taste of the most refined dimensions. The land is not for everyone. In fact, very few people like the thought of even passing through this place. Like all good things in life, the experience only grows progressively better with time, understanding, and acceptance. One thing I've found about good country is that getting into the land takes actual physical time. Whether it's a small strip of wild riparian corridor along Turtle Creek in southern Wisconsin or the awesome emptiness of the Grand Erg Occidental on the western edge of the Sahara Desert or the surreal interior of Iceland, time is needed to come to the heart of things. The Tongue is no different.

You must drive an hour south of Billings before you even reach a lesser road leading east past the Little Bighorn River and on toward Ashland. From here you wind another hour or more south before climbing up into the plateaus on either side of the road. Huge, eroded, crumbling walls of yellow-brown rock guard the entrances into this uninhabited land south of the Northern Chey-enne Indian Reservation. For what seems like a very long time you wander rutted trails in the red dirt that only grow narrower and bumpier and more dusty. Flocks of turkeys rush into the ponderosa. Deer are everywhere, along with pheasants and sharptails and small rodents that support a thriving community of raptors.

Once out of Ashland or Lame Deer or Birney or Lodge Grass or Sheridan in the south you are on your own. Water is scarce and what there is of it tastes of the oil and coal and other minerals buried in the ground here. A rancher might sell you some gas if you run out, but he will do so with a rueful smile that clearly says only a fool would travel this country without topping off his tank and carrying some more in a five-gallon gerry can. If you are seeking the center of this country you will put in some hard miles in your truck and then on foot. Once you find what you wanted, what the country has to offer, only then will the realization that the truth of the search was lying flat on the dry ground in front of you all of the time everywhere you went become apparent. That's good country, and you make the most of it whenever you can.

Another aspect of this land is that once you give in to the rhythms and the pace of the place, almost everything that occurs brings with it a sense of familiarity coupled with a feeling of appropriateness that seems to have coincidence written all over it. That's what happens when you throw off the civilized trappings of pedestrian madness and cruise on natural autopilot. The whole convoluted world down here is rife with coincidence zinging through a psychedelic atmosphere. Getting lost on several levels is easy and pleasurable. Coming back is the bitch.

That, too, is the Tongue, but even way out here the huge strip mines and a proposed railroad along the brown trout part of the river threaten the experience. Machines so big they could eat a dozen Buicks for breakfast tear up the ground with a subliminal rumble felt for miles. They dump millions of tons of coal into a long waiting train. When the sucker is full, another will take its place. And then still another. The mine is near Decker, which is itself nothing more than a small store-post-office that has an old brown dog sleeping on the front porch. Three seams of coal ranging from twelve to thirty-seven feet thick and running for miles and miles lie just beneath the surface here. Thousands of acres of colorful hills, bluffs, and coulees have already been leveled to mine the black stuff. There are more than two billion tons of bituminous coal lying in the ground. More than enough to power the USA for decades. I hope the hungry machines won't eat their way into the river, and the railroad is still years off, but people need to know that even rattlesnake, spider, and cactus country is threatened by greedy developers. They never sleep and they never quit. Like the coal trains, there's always another one coming down the line.

The Tongue River really begins along the east slopes of the Big Horn Mountains in Wyoming before curving and twisting 35 of its 265 total miles through grassy cottonwood-lined banks into the stark country of the Tongue River Reservoir. The river is much better fishing in Wyoming, looking for all the world there like a combination of the Beaverhead and the upper Clark Fork as it flows through ranching and farming land not far from Sheridan. There are browns in here, some up to several pounds. There are other trout, too. Wyoming terms the upper river Class I in the headwaters, or of national significance, and Class II farther down, or of statewide significance.

In Montana below the reservoir, the Tongue never reaches those lofty heights. Inconsistent flow levels that strand both trout eggs and fry along with large numbers of invertebrates curtail the numbers of naturally producing browns and rainbows that are both wild and helped along a little by judicious plantings. Also, the land is barren and desertlike compared to the emerald irrigated fields just upstream in Wyoming. This part of the river runs with a tougher crowd. Life is certainly good along the Tongue but it sure is not easy for anything or anybody. Along with the trout and the sauger there are smallmouth bass scattered throughout the river in deeper pools as far down as where the Tongue joins the Yellowstone at Miles City. There are also large numbers of suckers and other coarse fish.

During runoff the river may reach 800 cfs in Wyoming, but this influx of water is used to refill the reservoir. The levels in the river below the dam for the miles that contain trout vary between 100 and 300 cfs. This flow is augmented by cold-water upwellings triggered by the water stored above the dam. These springs are literally lifesavers for the browns and rainbows in the hundred-degree-plus heat of summer.

I have caught less than a dozen browns, never a rainbow, a few sauger, and a handful of smallmouths on the Tongue over the years. I am now convinced the browns can be taken with drys, but I have yet to take one in daylight. If there is enough light to read a book there is too much light for the browns, who hide beneath the undercut banks and anywhere else out of sight of predators like hawks and eagles and Lord knows what else. Taking browns during the day will come from working streamers down along the bottom as far into the dark banks as possible. This will take time but, browns being browns, eventually one of them will give in to predatory nature and hammer my fly. And I've devoted a lot of time learning about working streamers. Not as much as some fly fishers, but enough to advance my technique.

"I admire your expertise with a Bugger," laughed my friend over the telephone in response to my telling him about a large rainbow I'd recently taken on the pattern in a high-plains lake. Admittedly, there are several techniques that can make the difference between success and failure when using patterns like Woolly Buggers, Marabou Muddlers, Mickey Finns, Zonkers, and the like, all potential picks for the Tongue, but becoming competent with streamers is far easier than, say, learning how to consistently take trout on spring creeks or keep campaign promises.

Streamers are big-fish patterns, but to be effective a fly fisher must be able to recognize prime habitat, use appropriate casts and retrieves, select the right fly, and most importantly, think like a predator, because that is what you are seeking—the biggest trout of a given system. The top of the aquatic food chain. Those fish that devour smaller fish like sculpins, creek chubs, and other trout.

In no other fishing does having the right rod married to the proper line and leader combination count for so much toward taking fish. Too light a setup and casting the heavy patterns is work, at best. Mismatched line and rod will translate to wild casts, spooked trout, and a banged-up head.

Using streamers usually means flies from size 6 up to 2/0 with rods that can take a beating even when used with sinking tip lines in fast current on windy days along brushy banks. For rivers in Montana this can mean rods anywhere from 4-weights for streams like the upper Clark Fork or the Boulder up to 8-weights on big waters like the Missouri or Yellowstone below Big Timber. Too small a rod means tough casting, a sore arm, and often a broken rod tip. If you are going to err, err on the side of using a heavier rod with a lighter line, not the other way around. For example, use a 5-weight line with a 6-weight rod. And a nine-foot 6 is a better choice than an eight-foot. The heavier, longer rod gives you more casting and retrieving control, especially when working tangled, undercut banks.

When fishing streamers, usually for big browns, I never use a leader of less than 3X. I'm after big fish, often in runs of exposed roots and branches. There is no point in trying to play things cute. Any fish that spooks from these tippet sizes is too sophisticated for my heavy-handed approach. Leader lengths of between 6 and 7½ feet seem to work best, balancing natural action with control and strength. An improved clinch connects the streamer to the tippet. Some of my friends use a Duncan loop because of the more lifelike action it allows the streamer. I can't argue with them on this point, but the knot also has enough slack to allow for break-offs from quick, savage takes that shock the eye of the hook into the tippet.

Minor details, and no one has ever accused me of being a rocket scientist when it comes to fishing.

When weight is needed, split shot is preferred to twist-ons for two reasons: one, there is less abrasion; and two, a split shot that is tightly crimped will not slip up or down the line.

One of the prime attributes of streamers is that they come alive in the water. Tied on a long-shank (4XL) hook with bushy, feathered bodies and tails, often heavily hackled, the flies pulse in the water as they drift in a river's current. Even in the hands of an amateur, streamers will dance and bob over prime lies looking for all the world like a crippled minnow trying to survive a serious malfunction. In the hands of an expert the fly is deadly. During certain times of the year, notably autumn, a talented angler can take over fifty fish in a day's float, some of them more than twenty inches long. The strikes are often savage, and frequently, more than one trout will rush from bankside cover to attack the lure like a starving pack of wolves.

Another virtue of most streamers concerns casting. Although, because of its weight, it is not as easy or pleasurable to work as a small dry fly, the very nature of the pattern allows for sloppy presentations. The idea is normally to get the pattern as close to the bank as possible and then begin the retrieve. The best streamer terrain is often undercut and covered with dense brush — ideal habitat for secretive and very large brown trout. Often an errant or noisy cast will actually attract the attention of a trout, the *splat* or *plop* indicating the presence of perhaps a wounded minnow or a large grasshopper. Make such a ruckus during a hatch of mayflies and every decent trout for one hundred yards will race for cover and cease feeding for hours.

"Most of the time I prefer to fish across stream and then mend downstream in order to swim the streamer," says a friend of mine. "Don't be in a hurry to fish out the cast. Try to get big, long drifts, the kind that present the fly in front of the fish for a long time. Often the trout will hit the thing at the end of the drift as it begins to swing out with the current. You have to be ready at these times because the take is swift and you don't have much line to work with — it is all extended by the drift in the current. A lot of guys strip their line in too fast and zip the bug out of the trout's zone. They're wasting their time when they do this. Big fish will not often move far out for food."

This advice seems straightforward but will fly in the face of ninety percent of the information other anglers will give you, most of which recommends that you should whip the streamer tight to the bank and then strip it in as fast as possible before making another rocketlike cast and retrieve. There are indeed numerous times when this approach is deadly, such as in the fall for browns.

Although most of the discussion so far has centered on the fly's ability to catch brown trout, streamers also account for many big rainbows, along with good numbers of brook trout and even wild cutthroat trout. Browns tend to be more piscivorous (they prefer to eat other fish) than the other species of trout, but rainbows measured in pounds and not inches are often taken from rivers like the Jefferson and Green on large streamers.

There are two basic approaches to tying streamers — with weight and without it. Both styles have their proponents, with those in favor of weight stating that this helps sink the pattern down to the stream bottom, where the bigger fish hang out. Those preferring the lighter models claim their choice has more motion in the water, thereby enticing more trout into striking. When working deep runs or pools, use weighted bugs. They are about the only way to drop down to the fish, but there are drawbacks. When you fish streamers down deep it is difficult to maintain control of the fly all the way through the drift. The different layers of water and varying currents twist and bend the line, creating a good deal of slack.

A lot of trout are going to take at the end of the drift. They will chase the pattern all the way downstream and you'll never know it. You have to do everything possible to keep control of your line, including mending, stripping in slack, and just trying to imagine where the bug is and what it is doing down there.

If this sounds a bit like a psychic conjuring act, in a way it is. Watching talented fly fishers does resemble observing a wizard creating something from thin air (or in this case, clear water). Concentration and a touch of intuition are vital in this submerged form of angling. Even a vicious hit from a big fish will seem muted and subdued through the distance of several feet of water and a variety of current speeds.

As for the unweighted versions, their increased buoyancy creates a much more lifelike action in the water. A sinking tip line that has a ten- or even twenty-foot weighted forward section that drops the pattern down to the fish works well. A weighted line is often easier to cast than is a weighted streamer, which has a tendency to find the back of one's head on the forward portion of the cast, especially on a windy trip down the river.

Keep the tippet short and heavy, sometimes only four to six feet for the entire leader, and 1X or 2X, twelve pounds, in heavy, murky water. The fish hit hard and you'll be working through tangles and submerged brush and other debris. You want a tippet that has enough strength to handle these conditions. It's no fun losing flies on every other cast, and replacing them can become expensive.

Even with a pattern as effective as streamers, you cannot just haul back and fling the contraption out in the middle of the river and expect to hook a trout. The fish have well-defined areas that offer shelter from predators and the force of the current and also provide a ready source of food.

Undercut, brushy banks are ideal locations. So are drop-offs just behind gravel bars. Logjams and other submerged structure always hold trout. Sometimes deep runs over broken stream bottom are productive because they afford fish plenty of cover and the current delivers a constant supply of unsuspecting forage fish like sculpins and minnows almost directly to the jaws of the waiting trout.

Most anglers fishing the Bugger cast right to a target area and then strip right in. True, this sometimes produces fish, but allowing the bug to drift and undulate in the current is far more productive. Cast tight to the bank and then roll-cast toward the bank. Mend line. Do anything needed to get line out to the bug to extend the drift. On good runs downriver, I've drifted a Bugger through a hundred yards or more of holding water. This is deadly. The fish stack up in the feeding lanes next to the bank and a good drift always means a good fish.

Streamer fishing is big-trout hunting at its best.

Fishing the banks is best done with lightly weighted patterns and sinking tip lines. There is better action and a greater opportunity for the current to push the streamer beneath the bank, where the big trout hang out. For deep holes and submerged structure, use sinking tips and weighted flies. This is tough fishing, aside from the mental effort involved. Digging line and fly up and out of deep, fast-moving water takes work and at least a 7-weight rod.

After fishing through the drift, the best way to accomplish the retrieve that begins a new cast is to quickly strip in the line until maybe fifteen or twenty feet remain out in the water. Trout often strike this frenetic motion, assuming the streamer is a minnow fleeing for cover. Also, a 7-weight rod is strong enough to readily pull this amount of line from the stream and create a strong backcast that allows you to shoot the line forward to your next target area.

While many purists look down their pointed noses at this ungainly fly, serious seekers of big trout know and revere the Woolly Bugger's fish-taking qualities. Few if any serious anglers will be found working the water without at least a couple of the things stashed away in their vest somewhere. There are many theories as to why the Woolly Bugger is so effective: it imitates forage fish, it looks like stonefly nymphs, or it just looks like something big and juicy to eat—something too tempting for a big brown or rainbow or brook trout to pass up.

In Montana, where taking big trout is a way of life, any river guide worth his salt fishes a Woolly Bugger at some time during the season, often with his own unique techniques. There are as many ways to effectively fish this pattern as there are skilled fly fishers, but casual observation by the neophyte will reveal that certain basic truths and techniques are manifested by all successful Woolly Bugger devotees.

"Buggers are good any time of the year," says my friend. "They are the first thing I turn to when the action is not taking place on the surface. Buggers are the play at first in these types of conditions. They are always good for one fish, then I'll get cute."

Woolly Buggers are tied in a variety of color combinations, ranging from all-olive to bright yellow. The selection should be dictated by water conditions. A very general rule of thumb would be to use olives and olive-and-black combinations when rivers are running clear and at near-normal levels. Brown buggers work as the water begins to go off-color. The black tie is perhaps the most productive in cloudy or even muddy water conditions. These are only general guidelines, and as with all fly fishing, observation and experimentation are of paramount importance.

The most popular combination is a body of olive chenille tied on a 4XL hook, #2–8, with a black marabou tail, black hackle tied along the length of the body, and a black-thread head. Lead wire is tied in near the head for weight. Another popular tie, one that works particularly well in murky water, is all-black. A brown fly with a black tail, hackle, and head is also prevalent.

While you would think that an all-yellow Woolly Bugger would be an unnatural combination in most rivers—few prime trout rivers have indigenous populations of goldfish in them—there are times, once again notably in the fall, when large brown trout find the color irresistible. This is one color combination that seems to benefit from a cast and then a quick stripping retrieve.

The fame of the Woolly Bugger is all the more astonishing when one considers that the pattern is scarcely a quarter-century old. Developed by Russell Blessing in 1967, the fly is now as famous as its much older counterparts, such as the Muddler Minnow, Adams, and Gold-Ribbed Hare's Ear. Its inventor refers to it as "just another ugly fly" and suggests that it imitates the leeches of his central Pennsylvania limestone streams. Noted angler Barry Beck is generally credited with first bringing the pattern to the big, wild waters of the Rockies.

Blessing experimented with various configurations for a number of years before settling on the current design, which he also suggests looks a bit like a hellgrammite, the larva of the dobson fly. He had originally intended to trim the hackle short, but decided against this when he noticed the lifelike action imparted to the feathers when he breathed on them. Blessing's daughter named the pattern, and Vince Marinaro referred to the tie as "Woolly Boogers." Such is the nature of fame.

I've taken some big trout on a variety of streamers but have had my best results on Buggers followed by sculpins, then Marabou Muddlers and Mickey Finns. Personal bias is directly responsible for this listing. Working any streamer pattern properly in good trout water will turn fish. Confidence in a pattern is paramount.

One problem with working a streamer or large nymph in extremely fast current is that when a big fish takes and cruises swiftly downstream, the drag from the fly line as it is pulled through the water causes break-offs. A partial solution to this is to use a shooting line with a narrow monofilament core and a slick coating to cut down on friction. There is a loss in control especially when mending, but on many occasions the drift is so close to the fly fisher that the shooting line does not come into play until a trout hits. This method requires that the pattern work right along the bottom, and extra weight is often needed. This is easily applied with a dropper of less diameter than the tippet. The weight will pop off before the streamer or nymph does. Definitely not pretty fishing, but excellent for fast water found in places like the locomotive chutes above Slide Inn on the Madison.

When trying to run down information about the Tongue concerning trout populations and types of bugs I contacted MDFWP biologist Phil Stewart, who informed me that there was "the usual assemblage of insects present," including mayflies (I've observed *Baetis* in spring and fall), caddis, and fair numbers of dipterans, an order I've largely ignored in my fishing.

Known as true flies, dipterans include craneflies, house flies, and mosquitoes. They began to appear almost a quarter of a billion years ago, and modern forms have been identified in fossils of over 180 million years. They can be terrestrial, aquatic, and even parasitic. They are found in every defined type of water and are often an important if not crucial food source for trout fingerlings and adult fish. The larvae all look alike to me. Most fly fishers experienced with these creatures say size and shade is more important than minute body details. This may be the most productive stage to fish, but drifting these little buggers just below the surface on small tippets, especially along the Tongue, is not high on any list of things I really want to do right this moment. Some year I'll devote a solid ten minutes to the art. Sure, and maybe I'll volunteer for community service tomorrow, too.

Adult dipterans, the ones that bite and carry diseases, have one set of wings, a rarity in the insect world matched by only a few species of mayflies and some other nonmainstream types of bugs. The other wing set has evolved into devices that stabilize the skinny insects during flight.

Midges (chironomids) are the main dipteran for trout. They are present everywhere and always give me a hard time when they are present on Armstrong Spring Creek. When in doubt, I fall back on the Griffith's Gnat #18–24 that is my only salvation, while those with confidence progress with élan from larva to pupa to adult, the sizes dropping one notch with each stage. Where are my Buggers? When the stillborns, and sometime later the adults, are present, I've found that small hackled drys work fine. Blue-Winged Olives and small Adamses have turned a good trick or two on rivers for me. Favorite shades, roughly in some sort of empirical order, are black, brown, olive, gray, tan, and cream.

Mosquitoes (culicids) are not high on my list of insects to imitate. Most of the times they become prime trout food sources find me standing around a smoky fire or fishing somewhere else. Mosquito larvae have been responsible for some nice trout, notably some big brook trout on the Sand River in Ontario during the carefree days of my youth. Adamses imitate the adult well enough.

Finally, there are craneflies (tipulidans), and these have led to two exceptional days on the Beaverhead when that river's large browns and rainbows lost all of their studied sophistication and madly splashed and romped after the bugs with voracious frenzy. The river was actually easy to fish on those two brief periods of bliss. My favorite pattern is a Tim Tollett creation, called Tim's Spent Wing, in #4–8. His T's Crane Nymph in the same sizes is also a nice selection. Warm, humid summer days, or even during a light shower, are prime times for cranefly activity.

All of this talk about imitating small insects with fragile dry flies is nice and probably marginally seductive for far-and-fine devotees, but aside from the autumn caddis that turn browns, all other trout I've taken on the Tongue moved on streamers. Last spring was no exception. After fishing the Bighorn for a day, we bought beer, ice, food, and filled water jugs while watching a

shaking remnant of the Beat Generation gas up his battered
Chrysler Imperial outside of Hardin. The guy was translucent
white, and his bare right foot kept a steady 78-rpm beat going
on the pavement. This boy was way out there, had been out there
from the looks of things for a very long time, and could have been
into the euphoric properties of carbolic acid for all we knew.

With a sense of relief we headed east for many miles before
holing up high on a bluff in the middle of hordes of gobbling
turkeys and packs of barking coyotes. The next day, after trying
our hands at some spring-fed ponds that were troutless, Talia and
I struck off for the river by way of a twisting gravel road that
climbed up on a wide, brilliantly green grassy plateau studded
with waves of yellow wildflowers. The Big Horn Mountains were
purple in the hazy heat. A group of antelope pulled alongside and
kept us company while we motored along at thirty-five miles per
hour to the tunes of Lyle Lovett. We kept on driving and the prong-
horns kept on running for yards and yards that turned into time-
less miles. Distance did not matter, all of us were off to see the
Tongue.

And we arrived at the river. Talia caught sauger, made dinner,
then relaxed by a fire while I tottered off to flail away in the dark
as thousands of suckers and carp and maybe smallmouth plus a
brown or two rose to tiny insects. Midges? I stayed with my trusty
Bugger and caught a pair of small browns and bumped a sucker
or sauger on another retrieve. We broke camp the following day
and headed to Armstrong Spring Creek and then to a superb meal
at Chico Hot Springs. And that's part of the Tongue experience.
Whatever is offered, you take. Whatever you feel like doing, you
do. Pretty simple.

Perhaps this carefree approach to life is ignited by the ancient,
well-rehearsed rhythms of Tongue country that vibrate throughout
the eroded gullies choked with dry tumbleweed and across the
serene surface of the river itself. Consider that a ditchdigger not
so long ago unearthed a huge skull belonging to the forerunner
of today's bison, *Bison occidentalis,* while laboring south of Miles
City. The find was blackened in spots, possibly by "original"

Montana residents cooking chunks of juicy meat over a crackling campfire. This part of the Tongue River valley is known for producing quality, protein-rich native grass and probably did so way back when this one-ton-plus bison roamed the land. Maybe there were cave bears hiding in holes worn into the Badlands. Did dire wolves howl with an intensity we can only imagine? Were saber-toothed tigers running down prehistoric grouse of ostrichlike dimensions? I know—the mind of a child at work once again.

Closer to home on the linear time continuum, in the autumn of 1876, shortly after the Indians' victory over Custer at Little Bighorn, The Tongue River Cantonment was formed and Fort Keogh was built at the confluence of the Tongue and the Yellowstone. The compound was named after Captain Myles W. Keough, who died in the battle. General Nelson A. Miles, as in Miles City, was put in charge. Miles had led the capture of Geronimo in the southwestern desert and had also received Nez Perce Chief Joseph's surrender in the Bear Paws. Indians called the general "Bear Coat" because he wore heavy winter clothing and a round fur cap. Miles essentially ran Sitting Bull out of Little Bighorn country and into Canada, where he stayed until his surrender in 1881. In 1877 Miles marched his troops up the Tongue to the headquarters of Crazy Horse, where he started a withering campaign that finished off this band of warriors except for Lame Deer and his Minneconyoux tribe of Sioux. Miles took care of Lame Deer on May 7 of the same year. His work done, Miles turned his attentions elsewhere.

Ancient vibes. Murderous vibes. Revenge vibes. All mixed in with wild, unpopulated vibes.

Ornette Coleman ain't got nothin' on the Tongue.

After catching the brown and tagging the other on the caddis dry, I loaded up the fire as a hedge against the gathering cold, a touch of that old nighttime fear, and a wiff of loneliness that is also a part of good country and being on the road. I poured some Jack in the cup and headed off to fantasy land. Daydreams no longer included playing lead guitar for the Bonzo Dog Band or, even worse, becoming a famous novelist. More mundane thoughts were at work now.

Since bull trout were no longer fair game and Montana already
had plenty of brown trout and rainbow trout rivers, how about
stocking the Tongue with taimen? I know, I know. Seems far-
fetched, and I can already hear Jim Pruett thinking "I should have
cut Holt off at two books. What have I done to the company?"
Bear with me. I've done my homework on the species.

The taimen belongs to the genus *Hucho,* and its indigenous
habitat is one of the most extensive of any freshwater fish. There
are four species, including *Hucho hucho taimen* and *Hucho hucho
hucho,* also known as the huchen or Danube salmon. I wanted
to fish for huchen in Europe during a vineyard pilgrimage (the
recurring theme of good country weaves through my life like a
fine trout stream) in the early seventies, but somehow things never
clicked in that regard.

Taimen inhabit watersheds in Siberia, northern China, and
northern Outer Mongolia, terrain that rests along similar latitudes
as does Montana. Taimen prefer flowing water but also hang out
in lakes and reservoirs. These salmonids like waters primarily in
the foothill zone that have good oxygen content and are relatively
cold. In periods of high or muddy water, such as during spring
runoff, taimen retreat to bankside shelter. They are found at the
tailouts of large pools in the morning and afternoon and at night
move into shallow water. See, this is all coming together. They
have requirements similar to browns, much like the water found
along the Tongue below the reservoir.

According to some estimates, taimen may live as long as 100
to 170 years. Think of the sport these things would provide after
being caught and released eighty or ninety times. Taimen fishing
would put match-the-hatch madness on the Missouri or the
Henry's Fork to shame. And they spawn during runoff in the
spring, reducing their vulnerability to poachers at this highly susceptible stage of their lives. The largest taimen ever reported was
seven feet long and weighed 231 pounds. They are the biggest
salmonid species with the quickest growth rate of any freshwater
fish, and only sturgeon live longer. Forget tarpon. Bones. Permit.
Roosterfish. We're talking about a serious predator here.

Taimen are similar in shape to northern pike, though more rounded. Their huge mouths are filled with rows of razor-sharp teeth extended inward like a shark's. This is a species that belongs with rattlesnakes, black widows, cactus, insane turkeys, and lunatic fly fishers. Black spotting highlights a basic gray body that is nicely set off with a flaming red tail and anal fins. Dark vertical stripes tip all other fins, and the adipose is off-white. All in all, very chic.

Taimen would require huge patterns and 12-weight rods. High sport out on the Tongue. The fish eats prey that is anywhere from ten to forty-five percent of its own body weight. A 16/0 sucker tie should work nicely. Sixty-four fish species have been found in the stomachs of taimen, including pike, brown trout, Atlantic salmon, and pink salmon, along with a varying assortment of muskrat, mink, squirrel, and chipmunk. One taimen choked to death trying to swallow a puppy, and an eleven-pounder died trying to ingest an eleven-pound pike. Mongolian natives have watched grayling leap onto dry land to avoid becoming a taimen snack. This is my kind of trout.

Mongol folklore tells of a monstrous taimen trapped in river ice. Natives cut off chunks of the fish in order to survive a brutal winter. During breakup, the taimen, once freed, swam away. And they eat ducks with the same relish as a muskie does.

How can this concept fail? There is the large plunge pool below the Tongue River Reservoir. There are tons of fat suckers to feed on, plus an occasional clumsy rattler. The water is cold. The bank habitat is ideal. They are long-lived, predacious, and hardy. I demand that taimen be introduced into the Tongue River immediately. The MDFWP took away the bull trout. They owe me.

"John."

"Yes?"

"Take these right now and go to bed."

"Okay, but I really want taimen put in this river."

"Good night and sweet dreams, John."

"Sure. Good night."

Dreams being dreams, I drifted off into a sylvan landscape filled with the cries of loons and the howls of wolves. There I was, fishing, when carloads of teenagers pulled up to my camp. Ford Fairlanes. Studebakers. Super Bees. Vintage Mustangs. Youthful and carefree, dressed in midsixties garb, they unloaded cases of Hamm's beer, stoked up my fire, and proceeded to cook up piles of bratwurst and Italian sausages. Jan and Dean's "Deadman's Curve" blared from several radios. Sort of a portable stereophonic effect. I continued to cast to rising lenok (brown trout lookalikes) but the loons and the wolves were silent.

"Hey, mister. What's ya doin'?" they called.

"Fishing for lenok."

"Who?"

"Not who, more along the lines of 'what,' " I answered. "They're like trout."

"You aren't allowed to fish for trout anymore," one cute girl commented with flirtatious demeanor. I could be in big trouble here if my thoughts strayed from fishing. Steady there, big boy. "They're all gone, or most of them."

"Well, I can try can't I?" and I cast again, a nice shot quartering upstream, the yellow line falling quietly on the river.

"Mister, come over here and have a brat, then go back to sleep. This too will pass."

Hip kids. I did as I was told. Brat juices, mustard, and onions ran down my chin and fell on my shirt. A fine mess. Then I wriggled into my sleeping bag to the plaintive sounds of The Rip Chords wailing "Here I Stand."

A powerful sensation that I was being watched ended the idyll. Sitting upright, I saw strange, alien shapes not fifteen feet away and screamed in surprise and terror. The long skinny necks and oddly shaped heads shrank down into plump bodies, and an animated conversation of purts, clucks, and gobbles ensued.

A flock of turkeys, damn it. Probably on their way to the river for a predawn sip, and I was sleeping in their time-honored path. The flashlight's beam illuminated a couple of hefty jakes and some hens. They were not afraid. Curious and a touch put out, maybe. They slowly lumbered away, talking as they went.

I don't mind the dreams about winning new Jaguars or writing

*The Tongue River below the spillway.*

a best seller, but these sorts of downtime dalliances were too much. Time to head back home, so I loaded up the truck except for the fly rod. A couple more casts were called for. Six months would drag by before I saw the Tongue again next April. But I failed to move a fish. Not a brown or a sucker or a taimen.

Winding alongside the river, I spotted small groups of mule deer and some more turkeys. Up on the bluffs I pulled over and stood in the middle of the dirt road looking back down on the country. Low clouds spit cold rain driven by a blustery wind.

The Tongue and the surrounding hills looked lifeless. I know better. April is a long way off, but I'm a patient soul, particularly when this country is involved.

# SUN RIVER

Yes, cousin Steve and I were definitely in peak physical condition. The seven-mile hike along a mostly level trail from Gibson Dam to the confluence of the North and South forks of the Sun River had been a cakewalk. The scenery was magnificent, and a sharp breeze that whipped down from the peaks to the west and gained velocity as the air squeezed between a neck of the reservoir cooled our finely tuned systems. The warmth of the sun felt good baking the tops of our bald heads. Two quarts of water and a dozen double-chocolate-chip cookies later, I was ready to follow my companion down to the first stretch of the main river just east of the Bob Marshall Wilderness.

To say that the fishing here was tough would beg the absurd. Cutthroat and lesser numbers of rainbows fought for our offerings. Bushily tied Deer Hair Caddis drove the fish crazy. They were not large trout, averaging a foot or so, but they were wild and unsophisticated. Anything more would have finished us off. We were a bit woozy from the stroll in to this part of the stream.

The river was frigid and ever so slightly influenced by the lingering remains of runoff here in early June. Snowpack was down this year, and not much of the stuff remained in the mountains above us. The day was bright, the grass was green, the sky blue and filled with cumulus clouds. There were flowers and bees and some caddis. Ants were converging on cookie crumbs scattered about in the sand. All was right with this part of the world except

112

*The Sun River below Gibson Reservoir—good rainbow and cutthroat water.*

for my sore feet and Steve's sunburned back, but we'd been
through tough times before together.

The quarter-mile run of the Sun before the water slowed to lake-
like velocity at the head of Gibson Reservoir was jammed with
trout; it is perhaps 150 feet wide, with deep aquamarine channels
and plenty of boulders knocking down the flow—ideal habitat.
There were no footprints along the beach, and we guessed that
aside from those working and living at the guest ranch nestled
between the two forks, we were the first boys to cast over these
fish this year. Wilderness fishing in Bob Marshall country becomes
joyously easy and ridiculous at times. This was one of them. Anyone can catch a hundred or many more cutthroat and whitefish
and rainbows (but not bull trout anymore, as we've seen) in an
afternoon's casting. Hare's Ears worked. Buggers would work, but
one must draw the line somewhere in the sand next to this charm-
ing flow. We played like happy children for a few hours, then
laced on our hot, cruel boots for the march home.

Two days ago Steve had flown in from his home in Minnesota
in a Cessna 182. He was accumulating flight hours toward some
well-defined goal. Flying out to Choteau seemed as good a choice
as any. We secured his plane, motored to Augusta in the portable death trap (my truck), bought plenty of supplies plus large
ice cream cones, gassed up, and headed for the Sun.

We spent the first night at Willow Creek Reservoir casting for
fish we never saw, supposedly browns. The Front loomed in the
blue-tinted distance. In the morning we headed for the river, and
with some nosing around discovered an ideal campsite along a
little lane across from the main road. The place was tucked beneath
some Ponderosa above the Sun as it raced through a gorge below
the dam. While setting up our gear, Steve noticed a cinnamon
griz crossing the river a hundred yards below us, probably wandering down from Castle Reef country. The bear acted as if he had
winded us, because he twisted and turned his head into the breeze
that cruised past camp. Steve wanted, I think, to believe otherwise, and was obviously relieved when the bear headed up a drainage that climbed south through a dense carpet of pine near Scapegoat Ridge. Deer and elk sign were everywhere.

The following afternoon, what seemed long coming in turned gruesome staggering out. My legs were in shape, but I was operating on the feet of a sissy. They were blistered and burning, especially along the Achilles tendons. Steve fared only slightly better. Never reaching the truck for the quick run to camp seemed a possibility. Rounding a rock cliff and glimpsing Gibson Dam was a happy moment. My cousin mentioned that the sight of the ugly and aging structure made him feel warm all over. Obviously, the two of us were shot. Brain fade was coming on. We needed cold drinks, sizzling steaks, and some time to recover while reclining on air mattresses and sleeping next to a small fire. We were truck camping and had coolers and ice and all kinds of liquids and foodstuffs, not to mention an axe, a propane stove, and lots of fishing gear. The days where Steve and I shouldered heavy backpacks were pretty much a dead issue, shot in the ass of slumping middle age. But to even consider hikes of the magnitude often described by writer Jim Harrison in his column for *Esquire* seemed folly. To attempt covering twenty or more miles in tough country shouldering a well-laden pack was out of the question. That type of harsh business was best left to the pros.

Sure, Steve still talks a good game.

"John, wouldn't it be great to put on a pack and just keep on walking?" he'd say while soaking hot-pink feet in a cool stream, "We could go forever. Look at all those ridges. There must be lakes all over the place."

"You bet, Steve. Ready to move on?"

"No problems cousin," and he'd stand up slowly and stagger off muttering something about his "god-damned calf muscles."

So what? We knew each other's jive and we had indeed been through a lot together, and spending time alongside this river was more than pleasant. The Sun is good country, too, like the Middle Fork or the Tongue but with its own personality that is strongly influenced by the Rocky Mountain Front and all of the weather-borne bedlam common to the region. I used to miss chasing tornadoes back in the Midwest, that is until I discovered the linear hurricanes that constantly buffet the eastern slopes of the Rockies. If you are positioned properly, you can throw a coil of line up in the air and have it sail out over a lake's surface in a perfect cast. The wind blows so hard the surface is knocked flat. Whirling clouds of spray boil across the water. Float tubes tumble and bounce downwind like deranged beach balls. The truck rocks and shudders in the gale. The weather is at once exciting and frightening.

The Sun forms high in the wilderness. The South Fork begins in the Scapegoat below Trident Peaks. Rainbows and cutthroat up to maybe a pound take dry flies with wild abandon after runoff. The North Fork starts out below Pentagon Mountain behind Teton Peak. The fishing back here is excellent for wild rainbows, cutthroat, and a few brook trout. Both streams run parallel to the Rocky Mountain Front for more than twenty miles or more west, or behind the first ridge of peaks. All of the Bob Marshall is top-of-the-line terrain, and these two drainages are no exception.

Gibson Reservoir is about five and a half miles long if you are a bird, and a mile or more wide and deep. From the dam down to Diversion Dam, a large and lethal obstruction if you are floating, there are about two miles of riffles, runs, and deep pool water containing good numbers of rainbows, cutts, and brook trout to a couple of pounds on rare occasions. Figure on an average of about twelve inches or less. From Diversion Dam, water is siphoned off to both Willow Creek and Pishkun reservoirs. Flows below here suffer, as do the trout and the invertebrates, though at times there are some nice browns. Then the river breaks free of the mountains and runs out onto open, rolling hills. From here as far down as Simms there are more brown trout, though the floods of 1964 and 1975 did a number on the streambed, and heavy irrigation drawdown adds to the problems. There is some access, though most of the surrounding land is private and much of it is posted. A good map showing BLM holdings is vital to the fly fisher here. Along with the browns are a few brook and rainbow trout, and of course mountain whitefish. They're natives and they're everywhere. There used to be grayling, but they are extremely few and far between.

The rest of the river down to the Missouri at Great Falls is mostly a warm, turbid affair inhabited by the likes of northern pike (to twenty pounds), burbot, or ling and rough fish.

The geology of the area is as visually striking as any location in Montana. The Rocky Mountain Front towers above the plains. Miles of sheer reefs tilt and weave along a north-south line. Snow-covered peaks show in the distance. This really is where the plains meet the Rockies. The view is as spectacular as they come. This is powerful land. Even without the roaring wind, the energy is palpable.

Taking the road from the small town of Augusta (scene of a tempestuous and raucous rodeo that is unfortunately going slowly tourist and civilized) up to Gibson Dam affords excellent views of the overthrust belt. A large moraine littered with erratic boulders marks the edge of where a glacier flowed out of the Sun River Canyon. There are petroglyphs in the Indian Head Rock area. There are also numerous forest service campgrounds and fishing access sites. Entrance to the canyon is gained through a tight gorge that pinches down on the river. This eroded slab of Madison limestone forms the severe front of the Sawtooth Range. It is also the easternmost slab of overthrust rock. There follows a succession of similar slabs of Madison stone and narrow gorges all the way to the Mission Mountains, eighty miles to the west. The overthrust belt is characterized by ridges that trend north to south along upturned edges of resistant rock. Long valleys form along the lines of less-resistant features.

Bill Gardner of the MDFWP proved an invaluable source when it came to information about the trout in the Sun. He cited statistics that revealed much about the nature of the river. Above Elk Creek, which joins the Sun five miles east of Augusta, rainbow trout run from between seven and eighteen inches and one-quarter to two pounds. Browns average just under a foot and vary from .8 to 3.5 pounds. Below Elk Creek the figures are an average of thirteen and a half inches and one and a quarter pounds for browns with a top of just over four pounds and twenty-three to twenty-four inches, though Gardner stressed that these are rare. There are only about one-tenth as many rainbows that average a foot and three quarters of a pound, with a top of two pounds.

"The fishing is nothing extraordinary but can be good at times, like in the fall or after runoff," says Gardner. "There are springs and seepages in the lower sections that provide water for the trout. Some browns come up from the Missouri to spawn. You can count on *Baetis* and tricopterans, I'd use Elk Hairs for these, and there are sculpins which are good for browns."

Comparaduns are always good choices when mayflies are present. A recent article by Charles Meck suggests attaching a nylon shuck to the bend of a hook; he believes that trout "most often take nymphs and emergers, including duns, with the shuck still attached." This is when the insects are more vulnerable. They are having a hard time escaping the meniscus and are easier prey for trout. Quarter-inch or smaller strips of nylon are stretched so that they reform into tiny coils. These are then slid over the hook point up to the bend. Marking pens easily complete the simple process. Meck has experienced success with this approach in imitating midges, mayflies, and caddis. I've tried the caddis with a shuck and taken fish, but I think on this one day a fly roughly approximating a Chrysler Cordoba would have produced. At any rate, this concept bears further testing.

Although there is adequate water during the summer and into early autumn, there is also nice action with hoppers. The grasslands and agrarian fields surrounding the Sun after it escapes the gorge are prime habitat for grasshoppers. If you can find your way to the river on public land or obtain permission from a rancher to access his property, there is some very fine trout fishing to be had at this time of the season. Hopper fishing is among the easiest, most productive and exciting fly fishing found in this country and along many other trout streams in the state.

To practice upsream dead-drift hopper fishing is to persist in the woeful art of successful failure. Sure, a sedate bank-tight presentation of one of the many grasshopper patterns looks fine and proper, the way the terrestrial is supposed to be fished. Watching the bushy thing bounce downstream taking fish with a degree of consistency is rewarding. This is quite possibly the best fishing for above-average trout of the year for many of us. Yet in my home of Montana there are several individuals with little or no respect for fly-fishing convention. They eagerly flaunt their iconoclastic precepts with slightly twisted glee. Fishing the venerable hopper brings out a wicked gleam in their eyes. New patterns and techniques are evolving under the intense ultraviolet bombardment of a hot summer day.

All my angling life I'd heard that imitations of grasshoppers were the stuff of plentiful big-trout realities. With this lodged firmly in mind, I had vowed to work patterns matching these creatures devotedly throughout the summer and early fall of each new season. Over the years I'd become proficient at the upstream dead-drift hopper two-step. It took a fly fisher as far gone as talented trout sculptor Powell Swanser to show me the error of my pedestrian ways.

Powell is the inventor of the little-known but slightly famous Outlaw Hopper. He is responsible for many other things that have happened over the years in Montana, but I promise to leave that silliness alone, at least for now. He, along with his patient wife Tazun, also catches as many big trout—over twenty-four inches— as anyone around. His creation is a white-and-gray-and-red-in-spots extension of the basic grasshopper pattern. The thing is ugly and very effective. Gary LaFontaine says that the pattern is one of the most deadly stimulator patterns for big fish he has used. High praise indeed. All I know is that everywhere I've thrown it, trout have come out of nowhere, sometimes in very bad fishing conditions, to attack the hopper. Browns have nailed the thing at noon on a searing, blue-sky July day. Rainbows have fought over the pattern in snowstorms on Rock Creek.

Powell and LaFontaine are good friends and spend lots of their angling lives fishing the Upper Clark Fork. LaFontaine has done much to popularize the concept of skip-casting grasshopper patterns tight to banks to help draw the attentions of big trout through the commotion created on the water's surface. Powell has taken this approach a few notches further into the depleted ozone.

In addition to its unique appearance, one of the Outlaw's secrets for success is in its presentation. What follows is a distillation of the essence of fishing the Outlaw Hopper, gleaned over several beers at Swanser's home along the Upper Clark Fork River outside of Missoula.

"Presentation . . . ah, yes. I've had my share of ridicule," says Powell, who is not allowed to bring a dressed turkey into at least one bar I know of, but that truly is another story, maybe for *Soldier of Fortune*. "The presentation techniques I've worked up for this pattern are what I call Dirty Dancing. And this is no off-the-wall method but rather a bona fide system that makes this fly produce."

Powell describes the method using a typical late-summer, hopper-bank, deep-side-channel scenario. With a weight-forward 7-weight line and a six-foot leader including twenty inches of terminal tippet tapering to 3X or 4X, he suggests bypassing the tail of the run and concentrating one's efforts low and close to the belly of the pool.

The first sidearm cast sets the bug down soft under the far bank with a natural drift. The second cast hits slightly harder, and every two seconds the Outlaw gets a slight twitch. On the third cast Powell skips the hopper into the bank off the water's surface, and every three seconds he will pull it under water with a strip of a foot or two. If the pattern moves too far out of the feeding lane or foam line, he throws a quick loop, kicking the hopper back into place.

"If the big brown hasn't nailed it by now, I'm out of there! I back out low and careful, slip around and move to the head of the run. I'm down on one knee stripping out the line I need plus ten feet. Then I flip the bug back into the foam line and let the current take the bug downstream on the natural."

When the pattern has reached the end of the drift and is hanging in the current, Powell holds it still for three seconds before initiating a slow, straight, deliberate retrieve upstream through the foam line. The second cast is allowed to drift several feet farther downstream and then is retrieved in big, sweeping, S curves.

"The third cast is the one that has turned more than one non-believer into a follower of the true faith," says Powell. "The fly hits the hole two feet down from the foam and it doesn't stop bouncing for sixty seconds. I have had twenty-five-inch German browns do a complete cartwheel in the air trying to get their clammy little hands on the Outlaw."

If this fails to draw a response from the trout, hang a split shot on the tippet knot and double-haul to the tail of the pool, snap the rod tip sideways to break the surface tension, and bring the hopper back with rapid eighteen-inch retrieves. The deer hair and soft hackle lie back against the side of the body and the fly will make a complete revolution every three or four strips, creating a good deal of turbulence that imitates a wounded minnow — prime big-trout pickings.

"One more cast like this one should be enough to either incite a strike or drive the inhabitants to the next river," laughs Powell while he juggles a handful of iron supplement pills in one hand. Don't ask what these are for. You do not want to know. "If nothing has happened and you are convinced there's a world record in the hole, clip off the deer hair and pull out all the tail hair except for two on each side. Leave the split shot in place and toss a high one at the head of the run — throw a mend in the air. Bounce your new stonefly nymph down the trench right past the big brown's nose. Many times this is what the old spoiled one has been waiting for."

All of this sounds like a lengthy and complicated procedure, but with some practice the routine falls quickly into place. The technique is for *big* trout with the advantages of imitating not only a grasshopper but a minnow and both an egg-laying stonefly and its nymphal form. The Outlaw also approximates some large October caddis and the salmonfly that has its wild beginnings on the river just below Powell's home and works its way upstream into a frenzy as it turns the corner and blasts upcreek.

"The Outlaw Hopper is the John Deere tractor of the fly world," adds Powell. "It may not be the prettiest thing in the hay field, but you're never let down when it's time to harvest the hay. More than once I've tossed the Outlaw into the middle of a PMD hatch with the ten village idiots gobbling frantically and locked tight to a #16 imago only to have a twenty-four-inch granddaddy try to slam my big bug into the sunset."

Although Powell's method has proved itself several times over for me, most recently on a small east-slope stream where I caught a number of browns over twenty inches, there are some things to look for when hopper fishing. Just because hundreds (or even thousands) of grasshoppers burst forth alongside a choice trout stream all of a sudden one day does not mean that the fish will immediately begin feeding on them, casting all caution to the prevailing breezes. Normally, several days of the new food item crashing into the water and drifting overhead in noticeable numbers are needed to cause trout, especially big ones, to shift from whatever happened to be the dominant food source prior to the hopper breakout.

This is true of any change in diet. Trout are opportunistic by nature, but they are also extremely efficient feeding machines. To abandon a source of protein that is readily available in favor of one that is making its first appearance on a given stream is not calorically efficient behavior: The newcomer may be a transitory phenomenon of little dietary significance. Thousands of years of evolution have established behavior patterns that run on this fact (among others).

All the same, once fish do key into the availability of hoppers, the fishing can be fabulous, to put things mildly. Ask any western angler to list his best days on the water, and one of them will surely be when grasshoppers were flying everywhere and huge trout were gulping them down. This is a time of an angler's year when he can take trophy trout, sometimes in staggering numbers.

When hoppers make their initial appearance on the water, as I mentioned previously, big trout will not be seen feeding on them in great numbers, but a patient individual who knows where specific large trout are holding can sometimes entice the fish to take by creating a false hatch. This is done by experienced anglers dealing with a variety of insects.

For example, by casting and then drifting a grasshopper over and over a run where a trout is stationed, the illusion of large hopper numbers is created in the trout's mind, and eventually, if the casting is done cautiously, so as not to spook the fish, it will rise and take your offering.

This requires patience and will, at most, advance the time of the hopper a few days—time that could be better spent searching out locations that are experiencing bumper crops of the erratic creatures.

A certain section of river that was prime hopper water last year may be a dead issue this year. An overabundance of insects, one that created excellent angling previously, may also have devastated the insect's food source. Nothing to eat very quickly translates into a precipitous downturn in population. Conversely, a field and adjacent stretch of stream that was poor hopper fishing the year before may be awash in the insects this July. Only a little pregame research will reveal where you should concentrate your efforts.

Places that deserve a high priority are fields of hay, wheat, alfalfa, and similar crops next to streams. These insect magnets are topnotch locations, especially if a farmer's harvesting coincides with the emergence of the hoppers or crickets. Fishing at times like these can actually turn boring after a few hours because of its simplicity and productivity.

Because of the free-flying nature of grasshoppers, you would think that trout would be found throughout a river. This is not necessarily the case. Bigger fish are reluctant to leave their prime holding areas and expose themselves out in the open to attacks from predators. When casting, work the water running next to banks or along any other available cover, such as midstream boulders or submerged logs.

Hoppers tend to increase in average size as the season progresses. When in doubt about size after matching the originals proves unsuccessful, try a larger size before going down to something smaller.

One last thing concerning grasshoppers. Despite their natural buoyancy, using a fly with a split shot above the hook to sink it to the bottom always seems to turn a fish or two, and sometimes these are the largest of the day. The reason for this is that a few insects invariably become waterlogged or trapped in a down-swirling current and wind up bouncing along the rocks and gravel. Trout, already keyed to the hoppers, are unable to resist a whole-some meal delivered to their doorsteps. It is also quite possible that these drowned insects imitate small, mangled minnows or large nymphs. Whatever the causes, this presentation takes fish in a way that is similar to Powell's approach.

Hopper season normally lasts until the first hard killing frost of autumn. Even after this time, a resurgence of summerlike weather may trigger another "hatch," prolonging the fishing.

If for no other reason than for the sake of variety, I suggest tying a couple Outlaw Hoppers and trying out my good friend's unique approach on some notable grasshopper turf in your area. One-trick ponies are a bore. Live a little and don't be afraid to become a practicing heretic. And don't worry about the iron supplements. Powell just likes to take good care of himself. Isn't that right, Powell?

One aspect of fly fishing I absolutely abhor is competition. Who caught the most or the largest trout. That nonsense can swirl around somebody else. Certainly there is plenty of room for a bit of good-natured give and take. This sort of thing goes on be-tween my friends and me or my stepfather and me all the time. But the nasty bordering on wicked stuff that is becoming more evident on the water is awful, useless.

The worst example of this absurdity is the international world championship of fly fishing. Someone told me about this silliness, but I did not believe him. Now I've read about the contest. There are actually teams representing various countries that go out on a trout stream and try and see who can catch the most and largest fish. Hey, the good old US of A only finished ninth, but our team captain said we will do better in the future. I'm certainly excited and optimistic. Bring on the metal-flaked bass (trout?) boats and the referees in striped shirts carrying the certified scales and tape measures. Maybe we can get the sport into the Olympics. Do you think our guys (and gals) will have a chance at medaling? God, what foolishness. Where's my gun. Give me a break.

I much prefer the approach proffered by Nick Lyons in a recent "Seasonable Angler" column for *Fly Fisherman*. His words go to the heart of my disgust with things like the event described above:

"Going faster, we see less.

"Rushing, we miss everything except whether a fish chooses to lunch on something we've pitched in its general direction.

"That's not enough — either for the basic skills needed to catch a few fish or for the function of teaching us something about our quarry and its world, something that will lead us to respect it more, protect it more wisely, and pursue piscatorial pleasures with more understanding."

This goes to the essence of fly fishing for me, though maybe someday I'll find myself plumped down in some bleachers alongside the River Test chanting "USA, USA."

Don't bet on it.

Historically, the Sun has been able to handle huge amounts of water. When runoff peaked in 1991 at 9,000 cfs there was only slight flooding when the original riverbed was factored into the situation. The river is substantially larger than streams like the Dearborn or Judith or even the Smith, and comparable in size to the Marias, a river that drains the eastern slopes of Glacier Park.

"There are lots of problems with diversion, and in most years the trout are really hurting for water," comments Bill Gardner. "Ranchers are aware of the problem, and when they can they try and keep as much water as possible in the river, but their business is growing alfalfa and raising cattle. If the Sun had the water it could be a very good trout stream."

A familiar refrain heard concerning many rivers in Montana, including the Jefferson and the Tongue. And with the region in the throes of an apparent dry cycle in the weather patterns, rivers are actually shrinking. Even with increased awareness on the part of irrigators, there seems to be less water around, less water for the fish. The mean flow for the Sun in September at Vaughn just west of Great Falls is about 450 cfs. This year the level was 355 cfs. Lower readings were recorded for most rivers in the state.

Problems that plague the Jefferson concerning water diversion affect the Sun, too. Sections of the stream are almost sucked dry, and returning water is often warm and loaded with silt and chemicals. For many of its 101 miles, particularly below Diversion Dam, the river is unfloatable even in a canoe, according to Dianne McDermand, who has seen the river close up for a couple of decades.

"In drought years the river is nearly sucked dry below Diversion Dam. It's a disaster, and sometimes there is only between thirty and one hundred cfs in the river," says McDermand. "Here's a river that is totally impacted for ninety-seven of its one hundred and one miles either from being severely dewatered or silted, especially below where Muddy Creek comes in. Water temperatures often climb above seventy degrees. This is a desperate situation. Still, in spite of the incredible abuse the Sun supports a decent fishery. We maintain 'Hey! Here is a potential Blue Ribbon trout stream in disguise.' We know there are nice fish in here now. Think of the potential."

For someone, such as myself, who loves beef, the obvious solution is potentially a painful one. To help preserve and perhaps enhance prime trout fisheries, ranchers must be offered an alternative to raising the number of animals they are currently working. Less cattle means a need for less feed, and this translates into less water required for irrigating alfalfa fields, and this means more water for the trout and the bugs they live to eat. Ranchers will need to make up for the loss in income. This may eventually come from the state purchasing water rights from ranchers. In turn, this money may accrue from increased fees for fishing licenses and other recreation pursuits.

Basically this will boil down to whoever is willing to pay gets to play.

Another benefit to fewer cattle will be less riparian-zone damage from the heavy-hoofed tramplings of wandering animals as they move about the range in search of both grass to graze on and water to drink. Cattle can denude stream banks and trash a streambed in a matter of days, but the damage will heal itself given a respite from the bovine pounding. As things stand now, ranchers are only paying $1.92 per animal-unit month to graze their herds on BLM land. Market value for these rights ranges from $4.62 in the desert Southwest to as high as $10.26 in the Dakotas. The BLM would like to raise fees to market levels and then gradually reduce them as ranchers begin to adopt sound land-management practices that will restore wetlands, riparian zones, and native grasses. At the moment the public is in the position of subsidizing an industry so it can make a healthy profit at our expense. A most curious situation.

The river next to our camp below Gibson Dam more closely resembled the wild stuff above the reservoir. Rainbows, cutthroats, hybrids of the two, and even a brook trout rose steadily throughout the day to attractor patterns like Royal Humpies, Trudes, and Wulffs. Stimulators and Sofa Pillows in #6–10 took fish, and there were stonefly nymphs scattered sporadically along the freestone streambed. Early in the morning a Goddard Caddis produced, as did a Prince Nymph and some Hare's Ears drifted through the runs. Later in the day Hare's Ears in #12–14 bounced through the riffles and took rainbows up to fourteen inches.

As the sun slid over the horizon, Gray Elk Hairs in #12–14 took trout steadily, some of them around fifteen inches. The trout could come up from the depths of pools that must have been twenty feet or more deep. By dusk I switched to a weighted Bugger and worked the thing in sharp, erratic strips along cliff edges and across current seams. The trout, mainly rainbows, averaged close to fifteen inches with this method. For some esoteric reason not even known to me, I was fishing with an API reel. When a trout of over twenty inches slammed the Bugger and raced downstream, the reel spun with a sickening whine, then exploded. Parts of the thing clanged and clattered off the rocks into the water. True, the fish was in the three-pound range, but smoking a reel? The rest of the shiny black device found a watery grave in the heart of the turquoise pool. I went back to my Hardy Princess with a 5-weight line on a 6-weight rod, an ideal combination for this stretch of water.

In the three days we spent along the water, we caught trout that averaged about eleven inches. Although most were rainbows, there were some cutthroat, a few brook trout, and some hybrids.

I used to disdain hybrids (salmonid ethnic purity or something) until I realized that the meld of rainbow and cutthroat produces an exciting cross. The cutthroat's willingness to hit a dry when combined with the acrobatic nature of a rainbow makes for an excellent gamefish. Instead of watering down any of the better attributes of either species, both seem to combine smoothly, creating a trout that is fun to cast to and a good fighter in the bargain. Here's a stiff toast to the *Oncorhynchus clarki lewisi gairdneri*.

While Steve would cook himself in the sun to cancerous doneness, I would spend hours presenting all types of patterns to the trout in the large pool and along the runs and glides of the Sun. The trout just kept coming. I do not think I can ever get enough of watching wild fish take a dry and then feeling the pull and hearing the splash of clear water. This is pure, unsophisticated joy. Casting while standing in the cold current with a warm breeze drifting through the pines has intrinsic value. Peace of mind comes cheap on a good trout stream.

Bill Gardner mentioned that there were a number of arrowheads and tepee rings along the river. I learned through still more cursory research that the river was named by Plains Indians for mineral springs bubbling out of the ground near the headwaters. The Sun was known as the Medicine River. Those last two words were virtually interchangeable to the tribe when used in a healthful context. The Blackfeet referred to the Sun as Point-of-Rocks River.

The Hidastas tribe directed members of the Lewis and Clark Expedition to the mouth of the Sun. They told them that the river ran northwest through the Rocky Mountain Front and that another river ran the opposite direction, toward the Pacific Ocean, just a day's ride away. Earlier explorers to the area called this The Great Lake River on their charts. Notations on these documents indicated that the Pacific was reachable in eight days of floating. Lewis and Clark passed on this route partially because the Indians also said that the river was too shallow and rapid to be navigated. Horses would be needed to carry supplies, and the pair concluded that obtaining the animals at the headwaters of the Sun might prove difficult, a correct assumption as things turned out.

If the party had managed to come in over the Divide in the South Fork of the Sun drainage and then dropped down into the Danaher Basin in today's Bob Marshall Wilderness, they could have floated the South Fork of the Flathead to the main river and onto Flathead Lake. From there they would have proceeded to the Clark Fork of the Columbia and down to the sea in ships, as they say. This would possibly have been a more expeditious route than heading up the Missouri to Three Forks and then farther still up the Jefferson.

Whatever. Two hundred years of hindsight is wonderful. I can't imagine trying to fathom and divine the best way through the Rocky Mountain Front and across the northern Rockies. The easiest path looks to be around Marias Pass, but even that road has some extremely rough sections. Shrouded in glorious myth, the actual life of an explorer must have been far less glamorous.

Our time on the Sun ended all too swiftly, and soon I found myself saying goodbye to Steve and then watching him point his plane eastward. I had to head back over the mountains (Marias Pass) by way of the Blackfeet Indian Reservation and a few hours of float-tubing on a certain lake for big brook trout. Then it would be back to writing. Deadlines were approaching.

We had not worked the water below Diversion Dam for browns, but I would do so in the fall. The river was less than four hours' drive from home, and there would be more water in the stream by mid-September. That is when I had my best results in past years.

Heading home from the Tongue in October seemed as good a time as any to finish off the year's fishing on the Sun. As I turned north outside of Billings on the road to Lavina, a cold rain pelted the windshield. By the time I passed Acton and was running along Comanche Basin, the rain had turned to snow and was really coming down. The wipers could not keep up. Gusts rocked the

*The Sun River just below the confluence of the North and
South forks, facing the Bob Marshall Wilderness.*

truck and I was down to forty-five miles per hour and then forty. The snow was over six inches as I creeped through Broadview. The storm wiped out the countryside. All there was to be seen was the road and the piles of slop that pushed and tugged at the truck's tires. I hated driving in this stuff. Big trucks hauling in the opposite direction covered my windshield with a blinding spray that took long seconds to clear. My stomach was knotted and I was sweating. This was fun. A Ford Fairlane (Tongue River dreams turning real) passed me like I was standing still. I lost its fishtailing taillights in the snow. Rounding a bend in the Bull Mountains sometime later, I saw the Fairlane in a ditch, empty. Where was the driver? Vanished or never there to begin with? By the time I reached the turn to Harlowtown I was beat. The Ford was one of many vehicles that had lost contact with the highway sliding in the greasy snow. Wreckers were appearing out of thin air eager to make an early-season tow-charge buck.

Gassing up in town, I finally made it to a special spot along the Musselshell where I fought with the tent in the wind for an hour, gave up, and made a nest in a hollow of the river's bank with my tarp and sleeping bag. Austere to be sure, but I preferred this to a motel room—I hate those things. The wind howled and I nipped at some brandy. By late afternoon the weather calmed. I went fishing, taking, as always, some nice browns on Buggers. I cooked some brats (more dreamscape?), poured the remaining brandy into a pot of Ethiopian Harrar coffee, rebuilt a fire of twigs and small limbs on the ground next to me, and passed a surprisingly pleasant night waiting for daylight.

Sometime in the night the air temperature turned upward and the morning broke clear and quiet. I abandoned the nest (we all must do this some day) and headed to White Sulphur Springs, turning north through the Little Belt Mountains toward Great Falls. The wind was at it again by the time I reached Fort Shaw. I planned to work an out-of-the-way stretch of brown trout water above here. I'd stumbled onto the water while munching on a cheeseburger at Johnny's House of Fine Foods near Belt a couple of years back. The information was ground-truthed, proving quite accurate. Nice trout to a couple of pounds or so holding in pools and next to undercut, brushy banks. Familiar brownie turf.

The air was cold now, with flakes of snow stinging my face and hands in the Rocky Mountain Front hurricane. Winter was lurking on the northern horizon. I rigged a 7-weight weight-forward to counter the wind and strapped on an olive Woolly Bugger. Down in the stream bottom the air was almost calm and not as cold. There was a decent amount of water in the Sun. Irrigation season was over. The parched streambed of June took on the appearance of a trout stream. No bugs were rising, though, not even some *Baetis*.

Forty feet of line worked out over the dark water and the streamer crashed off the dry grasses of the far shore, plopping into the river. An exaggerated upstream mend, a pause to allow for appropriate sinkage, and a quick strip.

*Wham!* I love the feel of a brown when it streaks out from cover and attacks a Bugger. The trout tried to hightail it beneath the bank, but with 2X the fish did not make any headway. The brown was soon on the reel, running, circling, and shaking his way down-stream, boiling the water as he went. Another trout spooked along a gravel run. I could see the copper flash. I forced the trout to the surface for a better look and the fish jumped high, landing with a hard smack. The vision was stunning, probably not for everyone but certainly to a fly fisher. Transfixed, I watched the fish swim in the shallow water near me. Golden yellow belly, dark sides, silver highlights with black and crimson spots. A perfect brown splashing at my feet while the wind howled above us as the fresh weather blasted down along the Front.

For the next couple of hours I worked upstream, casting the Bugger along the entire far bank, swimming the sucker through runs and dead-tight to cover. The browns were everywhere, trig-gering my latent and only dimly developed predatory instincts.

Gone. Completely gone. The latest fine day on a stream is always the best of a season. Nothing over twenty inches, but the browns were plump, healthy, and plentiful. I wonder if they sold sections of the Sun at Brautigan's Old Towne Trout Stream Shoppe. I wanted some of this in my backyard. I kept saying out loud "Just one more," but I couldn't stop. Four hours from home, I'd pull in before ten, but for now I wanted some more of this action down here in the river safe from the storm rolling in above and the madness lying in wait along the highway.

It's hard to stop fishing in October when things are so good and spring is so far away.

# Conclusion: All Along the Watch Tower

*T*he river was tame by November. Where downed larch swirled in a stream gone berserk with melted snow and ice in late spring, the water was so low that I could wade to the far shore and fish a prime eddy where the Middle and North forks of the Flathead mixed. October's intensity was gone from my casting. Today was a bit of saying so long to another year spent fishing all over Montana. This was the first season that I'd considered the future, how many productive seasons might remain. At forty-one I hoped a bunch, but one never knows. There was no worry or concern over squandering the days. Time on a river is never wasted no matter how it is spent.

The afternoon was overcast but mild for this time of year. A Prince nymph turned up a couple of cutthroat and was half-heartedly bumped by some Lake Superior whitefish in the river. My response was less than intent. Wading across shallow shelves of gravel, casting along rocky banks, then bouncing the nymph along the streambed were automatic actions. One hundred and fifty days of fishing since March leads to this. Winter is a time to rest and regroup, to read and write and start to get worked up over the next season. I'll cross-country ski some, but not much, and I'll talk fishing over the phone with friends.

The loss of the opportunity to fish for bull trout is sad, for me and more importantly for the fish. I doubt that any of us will be casting to these char for many years, if ever, in Montana. I'm less than thrilled that fly fishers and other anglers are the target of the first broad steps aimed at preventing the extinction of bull trout in northwest Montana. Private industry and the forest service have conspired, done everything possible, to violate the spirit and intent of natural law in order to devastate the region's forests and streams, the places where bull trout spawn. Roads and clear-cuts funnel tons of silt and billions of gallons of runoff into fragile tributaries. Lake trout gorge on small bull trout as they emerge from their natal streams. Flathead Lake is a system in biological chaos.

Limits on lake trout are raised and you can catch tons of Lake Superior whitefish. No doubt some bull trout will be taken in the fray. Poachers will herd the fish upstream with pickup trucks, hauling the species out by the sackful. But we fly fishers lose another species in another drainage in the name of politics while the mountains and streams and valleys around us are destroyed by logging, development, and mismanagement. My guess is that westslope cutthroat trout will be taken away next. Then grayling. Montana will still offer fabulous fly fishing, but not for native trout. The rivers and lakes will have turned into game preserves, refuges of a sort, a depressing thought.

The process is obvious. Point a bureaucratic finger at anglers. Stir the poor bastards up. Create enough controversy and no one will notice the habitat destruction taking place all over the state. Simple solutions that fail to fix anything.

So we keep our favorite waters a tight secret until one day we pull up and find a clear-cut mess filled with mud and downed trees but no trout. Let's all hold our stash streams tight to our righteous little breasts and expend large amounts of energy uselessly whining in all the wrong directions. This makes sense to me.

A nice cutthroat pops the Prince and I bring the fish quickly in: silvery at this time of year and solid. Upon release the trout drifts out of sight, as quickly and abruptly as this year's bull trout season. This was the best season's fishing I've ever had, but I'm not really happy. Too much water was lost and more is going all of the time.

I realize that living long enough to enjoy fly fishing with my children is not really the issue. I think the wild trout will be history long before then.

The river pushes against my legs and I make one last cast . . .

# Notes and Comment

*A*rranging to fish the rivers discussed in this book is a relatively straightforward proposition, especially if you are curious, adventurous, and adaptable. The weather may turn awful, the bugs may bite while the trout won't. Just remember, you are never too far from a warm bar that serves strong ditches and greasy cheeseburgers.

Licenses are forty-five dollars for the season or ten dollars for two days for nonresidents. Be sure and grab a copy of the current regulations when you purchase your license. More specific and current travel information is available from Travel Montana, Department of Commerce, Helena, Montana 59620; 1 (800) 541-1447 outside of the state, or 444-2654 in-state.

Also ask for free copies of the *Montana Recreation Guide, Vacation Guide, Fishing Guide, Lodging Guide,* and the state highway map. You will find information on contacting fish and game regional departments and finding out about road conditions, as well as a thorough listing of licensed guides and outfitters in these sources. There are phone numbers for various local and regional chambers of commerce scattered around Montana, as well.

An excellent map of Montana, suitable for hanging on a wall (as too, are so many of us) is available from Raven Images, 1 (800) 237-0798. The forty-by-sixty-inch relief map costs twenty-five dollars and is worth the price. Two other maps that are quite good, especially for the road, are the Recreation Map of East

137

Montana and its western counterpart, from Western GeoGraphics, Box 1984, Canon City, Colorado 81215; (719) 275-8948. These are much better than the state highway map and only cost around three dollars each.

As for fishing gear, 2- and 3-weights for drys in delicate conditions are good sport. A 5-weight handles most dry, nymph, and streamer action on larger water. For truly big patterns and rough, deep water I use an Orvis Powerhouse 8-weight travel rod. This thing can handle wind, can work weighted patterns with sinking tips down deep, and has the backbone to turn big trout. Use double tapers for the small line sizes, and weight-forwards along with five- and ten-foot sinking tips for the 5- and 8-weights. Both Orvis and Teeny make quality sinking tips. I also like the floating Nymph-Tip by Cortland for the 5-weight. The line shoots well and the bright pink tip section helps visibility in bad light and broken water.

For clothing, plan for weather conditions of summer through winter when fishing in the spring and fall—hat, fingerless mittens, long underwear, sweaters—the works. "Fishing shirts" like the ones made by Ex Officio (Baja Plus) or Orvis (Bonefish Scrubs) and Marquessa have plenty of large, secure pockets, the material is durable, and they wash easily in a motel sink. They are worth what they cost.

If you are camping out, bring along a three-season sleeping bag, tent with rainfly, a good ground cloth, and a two-burner propane stove for quick pots of coffee or just plain old cooking when the wood is wet.

Felt-soled wading shoes, hippers, and chest waders (lightweight for all but the worst weather), and good rain gear are musts. As are sunglasses. I like the world view offered by Corning's Serengetis but also like the amber lenses found in glasses made by Bollé and Action Optics.

After an absence of more than a decade, I have returned to the dedicated ranks of fly tiers who believe in the sacred right to salvage fur and feather from road kills. I tie all my flies now, and this has added a good deal of pleasure to my fishing (and apparent confusion to the fish). Taking equipment on the road to match a unique local bug is also worthwhile and really does improve your results, especially when it comes to fooling the big fish. I throw dark blue dun, medium cree, brown, grizzly, and sandy dun necks in a soft-sided traveler's briefcase such as those offered by L.L. Bean in its catalogue luggage section. Spencer Hackles, 100 Deemer Creek Road, Plains, Montana 59859, (406) 826-3644, sells excellent feathers, especially in the brown shades, at reasonable prices. Right now they are as good a buy as there is on the market. Streamer, nymph, and dry-fly hooks, an assortment of preferred feathers, furs, threads, and a smattering of stuff like Flashabou or gray foam rubber for ant bodies is crammed in my bag.

Being a lover of toys, I have also found three items that are great for the road. Cortland's Supreme 3 fly-tying vise has three jaws, is easily adjustable, and costs less than fifty dollars. A short length of one-by-twelve wood board serves as a base. Another acquisition is a set of three tying scissors from Dr. Slick of Dillon, Montana. This trio covers the range of needs presented by the multitude of patterns we use. These tools are an artful amalgam of brass and steel. They come in a foam-padded case, so they are easy to pack.

The Tote 'N Float is a cross between a float tube and an Avon raft and has many of the advantages of both, including maneuverability, portability, and cost. You sit in the craft on a comfortable seat with chest waders and fins, as in a float tube, but ride well above the water, as in a raft. There is a set of small oars and room in back to pack judiciously for a day or several of downstream-floating and camping. It is well designed, solidly constructed, and stable in rough water, and I've floated the thing on the Middle Fork of the Flathead in rough chop with ease. It is seven feet long, weighs a touch over twenty pounds, and has straps on its carrying case for packing into off-road water. A nice toy and tool that runs a bit over five hundred dollars. More information is available by calling 1 (800) 858-1682.

## Middle Fork of the Flathead River, Swan River, Blackfoot River

Further information is available by calling 1 (800) 338-5072 (this and the numbers that follow are travel-related information sources). Paul Roos operates PRO, a respected outfitting operation in the state and can guide you on the Blackfoot. He can be reached at (406) 442-5489, 1630 Leslie, Helena, Montana 59601. Grizzly Hackle in Missoula offers just about all a fly fisher needs to chase trout. Call (406) 721-8996. There are many restaurants, motels, and hotels, along with stores selling most everything in this busy town.

Glacier Raft Company offers float trips down the Middle Fork. Call 1 (800) 332-9995, or write 6 Going-to-the-Sun Road, West Glacier, Montana 59936. Food, lodging, and anything else you may need is available in the towns of Kalispell, Bigfork, and White-fish. Snappy Sports Senter in Kalispell, (406) 257-7525, 1400 Highway 2 East, has all sorts of fishing and related gear.

Lakestream Flyfishing Company, operated by George Widener, has evolved into one of the finest shops in the state. You can find there a good supply of what you need to fish around the area. George is also a quality guide for the region. The shop is located at 15 Central Avenue, Whitefish, Montana 59937; (406) 862-1298.

For the Swan River, you should plan on exploring on your own for best results. You could also check in with Fish, Wildlife and Parks in Kalispell at (406) 752-5501. Food and lodging are available here and there along the Swan Highway and in Seely Lake, located about twenty miles south of the Swan divide.

## Jefferson River

Further information is available by calling (406) 846-1943. Frontier Anglers, 680 North Montana Street, Dillon, Montana 59725, (406) 683-5276, and Robert Butler Outfitting Company, Box 303, Twin Bridges, Montana 59754, (406) 684-5773, can float you on this water.

# Tongue River

You will be able to scrounge up some more travel information by calling (406) 665-1671, but not many people fish for trout below the dam. Sheridan, just beneath the border in Wyoming, has food and lodging. The Bighorn River is a couple hours west of the Tongue, and you might as well enjoy yourself on this classy but crowded water. Gordon and June Rose of Quill Gordon Fly Fishers are generous with their knowledge of the Bighorn and with their time. They may be reached at Box 597, Fort Smith, Montana 59035; (406) 666-2253. The Lariat Motel, run by Fay McCoy, 709 North Center, Hardin, Montana 59034; (406) 665-2683, is a good place to stay to fish the Bighorn or to recover from the Tongue. The Chat and Chew next door has filling breakfasts and even larger box lunches.

# Sun River

For further information, call 1 (800) 527-5348. The towns of Choteau and Augusta have food and lodging and just about anything else you may need. For the stout of heart, arm yourself with a copy of Montana's stream access law and approach ranchers along the river with a big smile and a very friendly disposition. Ask politely for permission to fish the river along their land. If they say "No!," keep smiling, say "Thanks anyway!" and make a sedate retreat.

# Further Reading

The following titles offer more information on Montana or will provide pleasant diversion when the fishing is out of shape.

*The Dry Fly: New Angles,* by Gary LaFontaine, has one hell of a lot of information and wisdom about fishing in Montana and other places (Greycliff Publishing Company, 1990).

*Finnegan's Wake,* by James Joyce. Just kidding.

*The Fishing Doctor,* by Robert F. Jones, is a fun book filled with facts, and it's waterproof to boot (Villard Books, 1992).

*Fly Fishing the South Platte River: An Angler's Guide,* by Roger Hill, gives an excellent sense of the rhythm and technique required to successfully work difficult water under many trying conditions (Pruett Publishing Company, 1991).

*Fly Tying Made Clear and Simple,* by Skip Morris, gives solid tying information for novices and veterans alike (Frank Amato Publications, 1992).

*A Hunter's Road,* by Jim Fergus, is an honest book by a talented writer (Henry Holt & Company, 1992).

*Mayflies, the Angler, and the Trout,* by Fred Arbona, is one of the best books on the subject of these delicate little bugs (Nick Lyons Books, 1989).

*Montana Time,* by John Barsness, is a gentle, thoughtful book about fishing by someone who loves the state, too (Lyons & Burford, Publishers, 1992).

142

*Native Trout of North America,* by Robert H. Smith, is a classic (or should be) about various species and subspecies of the salmonid clan (Frank Amato Publications, 1984).

*The Pocket Doctor,* by Stephen Bezruchka, M.D., for ailments of a more drastic sort than those covered in *The Fishing Doctor,* above (The Mountaineers Books, 1992).

*Poul Jorgensen's Book of Fly Tying,* by Poul Jorgensen, has a wealth of tying information for all levels of tiers (Johnson Books, 1988).

*Snake River Country,* by Bruce Staples, has excellent photos and tying instructions, along with the histories of many of the West's best patterns (Frank Amato Publications, 1992).

*Tourist Season,* by Carl Hiaasen, takes place in Florida but may have some applications up here in Montana (Warner Books, 1987).

*A Voice Crying in the Wilderness (Vox Clamatis in Deserto),* by Edward Abbey, is a collection of thoughts, comments, and observations by the late champion of our wild lands (St. Martin's Press, 1989).

# INDEX

145